The Land and People of

AFGHANISTAN

PORTRAITS OF THE NATIONS SERIES

The Land and People of®
AFGHANISTAN

by Mary Louise Clifford

J. B. LIPPINCOTT   NEW YORK

To my mother

Country maps by Susan M. Johnston/Melissa Turk & The Artist Network.

Every effort has been made to locate the copyright holders
of all copyrighted photographs and to secure the necessary
permission to reproduce them. In the event of any questions arising
as to their use, the publisher will be glad to make necessary
changes in future printings and editions.

THE LAND AND PEOPLE OF
is a registered trademark of
Harper & Row, Publishers, Inc.

The Land and People of Afghanistan
Copyright © 1989 by Mary Louise Clifford
Printed in the U.S.A. All rights reserved.
For information address J. B. Lippincott Junior Books,
10 East 53rd Street, New York, N.Y. 10022.

Library of Congress Cataloging-in-Publication Data
Clifford, Mary Louise.
    The land and people of Afghanistan / by Mary Louise Clifford
      p.   cm. — (Portraits of the nations series)
    Bibliography: p.
    Includes index.
    Summary: Introduces the history, geography, people, culture,
government, and economy of the Central Asian nation that has had a
history of invasion and conquest by its powerful neighbors.
      ISBN 0-397-32338-7 : $.   ISBN 0-397-32339-5 (lib. bdg.) : $
      1. Afghanistan—Juvenile literature.   [1. Afghanistan.] I. Title.
    II. Series.
DS351.5.C56 1989   88-21419
958′.1—dc 19   CIP
                                                                  AC

                    10 9 8 7 6 5 4 3 2 1
                              First Edition

Contents

THE WORLD

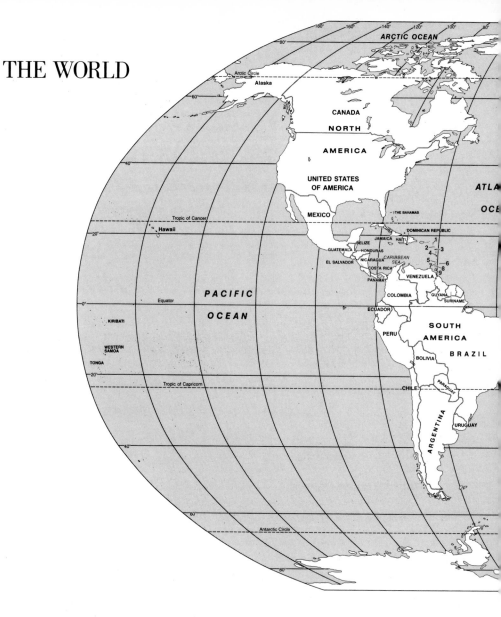

This world map is based on a projection developed by Arthur H. Robinson. The shape of each country and its size, relative to other countries, are more accurately expressed here than in previous maps. The map also gives equal importance to all of the continents, instead of placing North America at the center of the world. *Used by permission of the Foreign Policy Association.*

Legend

——— International boundaries

········· Disputed or undefined boundaries

Projection: Robinson

0	1000	2000	3000 Miles

0	1000	2000	3000 Kilometers

Caribbean Nations

1. Anguilla
2. St. Christopher and Nevis
3. Antigua and Barbuda
4. Dominica
5. St. Lucia
6. Barbados
7. St. Vincent
8. Grenada
9. Trinidad and Tobago

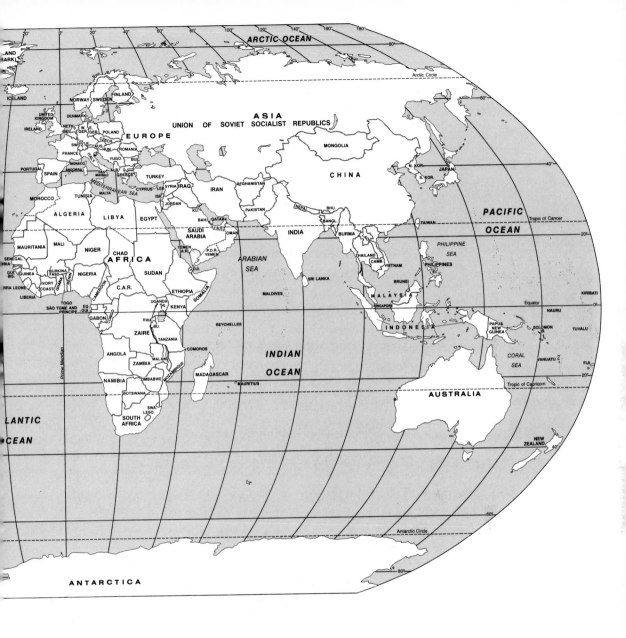

Abbreviations

ALB.	—Albania	
AUS.	—Austria	
BANGL.	—Bangladesh	
BEL.	—Belgium	
BHU.	—Bhutan	
BU.	—Burundi	
BUL.	—Bulgaria	
CAMB.	—Cambodia	

C.A.R.	—Central African Republic
CZECH.	—Czechoslovakia
DJI.	—Djibouti
E.GER.	—East Germany
EQ. GUI.	—Equatorial Guinea
GUI. BIS.	—Guinea Bissau
HUN.	—Hungary
ISR.	—Israel

LEB.	—Lebanon
LESO.	—Lesotho
LIE.	—Liechtenstein
LUX.	—Luxemburg
NETH.	—Netherlands
N. KOR.	—North Korea
P.D.R.–YEMEN	—People's Democratic Republic of Yemen

RWA.	—Rwanda
S. KOR.	—South Korea
SWA.	—Swaziland
SWITZ.	—Switzerland
U.A.E.	—United Arab Emirates
W. GER.	—West Germany
YEMEN A.R.	—Yemen Arab Republic
YUGO.	—Yugoslavia

Mini Facts

OFFICIAL NAME: Republic of Afghanistan

LOCATION: Between the Middle East and South Asia, astride the Hindu Kush mountains, with the Soviet Union to the north, China at the northeast tip, Pakistan to the east and south, and Iran to the west. The latitude and climate are about the same as that of Texas, except that Afghanistan has very high mountains.

AREA: 251,773 square miles. The country's size is similar to that of Texas. Its extreme length from west to east is 770 miles; its greatest width from north to south is 550 miles.

CAPITAL: Kabul (probably over 2 million people, over half of whom are displaced persons).

POPULATION: Between 15 million and 17 million, of whom 4 million to 5 million are refugees outside the country.

MAJOR LANGUAGES: Pushtu is the language of the largest tribal group and is spoken through southern and eastern Afghanistan. Dari Persian (called *Farsi* in Afghanistan) predominates in the cities and in the western part of the country. About twenty languages or dialects are spoken, but almost all Afghans are bilingual, and four fifths of them speak either Pushtu or Farsi.

RELIGION: Islam (four fifths Sunni; one fifth Shiah).

TYPE OF GOVERNMENT: Under communist control, a socialist autocracy.

HEAD OF STATE: President of the Revolutionary Council.

HEAD OF GOVERNMENT: Prime minister. (The chairman of the People's Democratic Party of Afghanistan has the real power.)

LEGISLATURE: Nonelected Revolutionary Council.

ADULT LITERACY: 12 percent.

LIFE EXPECTANCY: Male, 40; female, 41.

AVERAGE PER CAPITA INCOME: $167 per year.

MAIN PRODUCTS: Cotton, wheat, fruits, wool, hides, karakul pelts, textiles, carpets, cement, natural gas, minerals.

SOURCES: U.S. State Department Bureau of Public Affairs, *Afghanistan* (U.S. GPO, Washington, DC: July 1986)

The World Almanac and Book of Facts 1987
U.S. Bureau of the Census

Democratic Government of Afghanistan, "Report on the Socio-Economic Situation; Development Strategy Assistance Needs," May 1983. Prepared for the World Bank.

Spelling and Pronunciation

Wherever possible, common nouns from Arabic, Persian, or Pushtu have been spelled according to Webster's New International Dictionary.

The spelling of proper nouns in Afghanistan is a confusing business. No complete gazetteer exists, and the reader who pursues his interest in the country by further reading will find each author using a different system. For the sake of consistency and easy reading, spellings throughout this book are as near as possible to the sounds of the Afghan names as the Afghans pronounce them. Other familiar spellings have been indicated in parentheses, e.g., Ramazan (Ramadan), Pushtun (Pakhtun, Pathan), Uzbek (Uzbeg), etc.

The following rules of thumb for spelling and pronunciation have been followed throughout:

1. The sound of "a" is always "ah," e.g. (Ah)fgh(ah)nist(ah)n, K(ah)-bul, Gh(ah)zni, etc.

2. The letter "i" is generally pronounced as a long "e," as in the word "see." E.g. Ghazni is pronounced Ghahznee.

3. The use of "e" has been eliminated except in words having the sound of "e" as in "pet," e.g. Herat, Helmand.

4. The "u" has been used rather than "a" or "o" in words that are often spelled with either. The sound of this "u" is the "oo" sound of "foot." E.g. Pushtu rather than Pashto, Puhantun (Pohantoon), Khurasan (Khorasan).

5. "K" is used in preference to "Q" in names often spelled with either, since the pronunciation is a hard "k." E.g. Kandahar (Qandahar), Kunduz (Qunduz), Kizil Kala (Qizil Qala), etc.

6. The "ay" is used rather than "ai" or "ei" in words that should be pronounced like "hay." E.g. Sulayman, Husayn.

7. When "ai" is used, it is pronounced as a long "i," as in "high," e.g. Ghilzai, Sadozai.

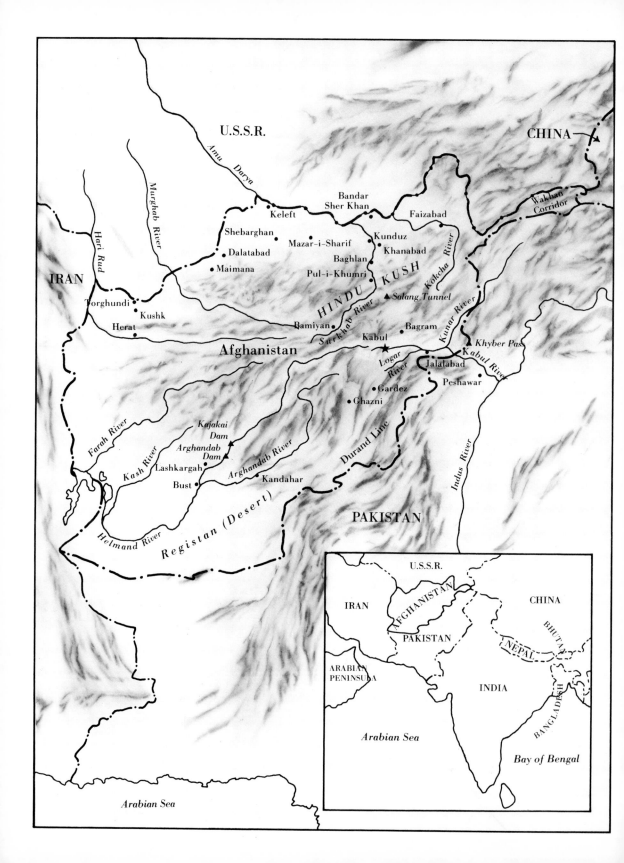

CHAPTER I

The Struggle for Autonomy

In 1747, not quite thirty years before the thirteen American colonies declared their independence, a new kingdom called Afghanistan was created in the mountains and plains that lie between Persia (today called Iran) and the Indian subcontinent. The name "Afghanistan" had not existed before that time, but the area embraced by the new kingdom had in earlier centuries suffered repeated conquest and invasion by its neighbors and had known many rulers.

In the centuries before 1500, trade between the Mediterranean and the East passed overland on the backs of pack animals in long caravans, and what is today Afghanistan lay astride the ancient trade routes. Long before Columbus discovered America, the merchandise of China and Mongolia moved along the Great Silk Route, through the northern

· 1 ·

plains of Afghanistan, and across the high passes to India or west to Baghdad and the Mediterranean. Consequently, the great rulers of those earlier centuries competed for control of both the open plains and the mountain passes that were the highways of commerce.

Three hundred years before the birth of Christ, Alexander the Great led his Macedonian Greeks through the Hindu Kush, the mountains that dominate modern Afghanistan, in his conquest of Central Asia and northwest India. Later, Indian rulers gained control of the country south of the Hindu Kush, while Central Asian nomads pushed into the northern plains and the Persians encroached from the west—a pattern that would be repeated many times.

Arab armies swept across the country in the seventh century, bringing the Moslem faith that would eventually give the Afghan people a unified religious outlook.

In the tenth century the most powerful kingdom in the area was actually centered in the Afghan city of Ghazni, with its rulers supreme all the way from Persia in the west to the Ganges River in India. They were in turn destroyed in the thirteenth century by the Mongolian horsemen of Genghis Khan. It was to the court of his son Kublai Khan that Marco Polo traveled when he went with his father and uncle from Venice along the Great Silk Route to visit far Cathay.

In the fourteenth century Turkish hordes led by Tamerlane swept over the Hindu Kush into India. Another leader of mixed Turkish and Mongol descent, Babur, conquered the Afghans in 1504 and moved on into India two decades later to found the Moghul dynasty.

But far to the west, on the Atlantic coast, new technology for navigating the oceans had already begun to change the world. The Portuguese developed ships that could sail both before and against the wind, and as an age of exploration began, trade shifted to the seas. The passes of the Hindu Kush were no longer on the main routes of commerce, but became instead the isolated borderlands over which the rulers of Russia, Persia, and India struggled as great colonial empires were formed.

It was from service in a Persian army that an able Afghan chief named Ahmad Khan Sadozai broke away during a revolution and founded modern Afghanistan.

His rise to power did not end the turbulence. Bits and pieces of his kingdom were snatched by his neighbors, Russia and the British rulers of India, who competed for control of Afghanistan for more than a century. Only in 1921 did the Afghan monarch regain control of his country's foreign affairs.

A brief fifty years of complete sovereignty were all Afghanistan enjoyed. The monarchy was overthrown in 1973, and in 1978 pro-Soviet leftists seized power after a bloody military coup. Quarreling among the radicals and growing opposition from tribal and religious leaders led to a massive invasion by Soviet troops in 1979 to impose a hand-picked communist government. Once again the Afghans had to struggle for their independence against their more powerful neighbors.

In 1988 the Soviets conceded that they could not defeat the Afghan resistance and began a military withdrawal, leaving behind great political uncertainty, a decimated population, and a devastated countryside.

A Dry and Rugged Land

Afghanistan straddles a natural mountain barrier between the Middle East and the Indian subcontinent, with Iran on the west, the U.S.S.R. to the north, and Pakistan to the east and south. Little rain falls, and there is no direct outlet to the sea.

The heart of the country is the Hindu Kush, a massive mountain range that is part of a great chain that includes the Himalayas, the Pamirs, and the Karakorum. These break up in the far northeast corner of Afghanistan into the Hindu Kush. This range continues westward, with Afghanistan laid over it like an oak leaf. The stem of the leaf is the high, narrow Wakhan Corridor, which touches China at its eastern end. The Hindu Kush and its subsidiary ranges are the ribs of the leaf, fanning out over Afghanistan and dominating the entire country. Along

An Afghan man, wearing his national dress, looks down on the main highway between Kabul and the Khyber Pass. This route follows the Kabul River through deep gorges in the Sulayman Mountains. United Nations

the fringes of the leaf are treeless plateaus, windswept plains, and sun-baked desert, which Afghanistan shares with its three neighbors.

In the northeast corner of Afghanistan the highest peaks of the Hindu Kush rise to more than 20,000 feet (6,000 meters) and are perpetually snowcapped above 13,000 feet (4,000 meters). The range continues westward at ever-diminishing heights until it fades out in a series of low ridges at the Iranian border some 700 miles (1,100 kilometers) away.

For centuries the passes through these mountains have served as the gateway from the north to India. They are rugged and tricky, but not a complete barrier. One of the high passes, the Salang, has a paved road and tunnel through it, making it passable year round in spite of the snow. The trails through the other passes can generally be crossed by pack animals from May to October.

The country's eastern border with Pakistan lies astride a much lower range of mountains than the Hindu Kush, running for a thousand miles along the crest of the Sulayman Range. Until recently, Afghanistan's rugged terrain isolated the country from the outside world because the approaches to its neighbors were limited by primitive modes of transport and impossibly rough roads. One of the most dramatic changes of the 1970s was the completion of a network of excellent highways that circle the country, linking Afghanistan's main cities to one another and to bordering countries.

Part of this network was built with American aid and contractors, but the bulk of it was built by the Soviet Union, including the all-weather Salang Tunnel through the northern mountains and a bridge across the Amu Darya River to make rapid transportation by rail and motor vehicle possible between the two countries. This road network proved of great strategic importance in the struggle for control of Afghanistan in the 1980s.

Because Afghanistan lies in a belt of desert that stretches all the way around the world near the latitude of the Tropic of Cancer, rainfall throughout the country averages no more than 11 or 12 inches yearly (27 to 30 centimeters). Only an eighth of the land is tillable; a third of it grows grass sufficient to sustain livestock, and two fifths of the country is either too dry or too mountainous for agriculture.

The mountain ranges catch the little moisture that falls, mostly in the form of winter snows. Without the snowmelt that feeds the mountain streams, the country would be desolate, for these streams provide irrigation water for farming and determine the locations of the villages, towns, and cities. The areas of Afghanistan that are not watered by river systems are too dry to be productive, and support only scant numbers of herdsmen on a seasonal basis.

Although the country is divided for administrative purposes into twenty-nine provinces of roughly similar size, many of these are bleak, barren, and very thinly populated. The centers of agriculture, commerce, and industry are all associated with four major river systems.

The Amu Darya Valley and Plain

Some 700 miles (1,100 kilometers) of Afghanistan's boundary with the U.S.S.R. are formed by the main channel of the Oxus River, which the Afghans call the Amu Darya. To the north are four Central Asian republics of the Soviet Union—Turkmenistan, Tajikistan, Kirghizia, and Uzbekistan, whose citizens are of the same ethnic stock as many of the people of northern Afghanistan.

The Amu Darya rises in the high mountains of the Wakhan Corridor (a political boundary drawn in 1895 to separate British India from Russia). The river's tributaries water the several provinces north of the Hindu Kush, which are inhabited by Turkish-speaking peoples and are consequently often called Afghan Turkistan. The course of the Amu

Darya skirts a high plateau punctuated by long valleys, principally those of the Kokcha and Kunduz tributaries, and wide stretches of fertile land that require regulated water supplies to make them productive.

Extensive irrigation works existed here before the thirteenth century, when they were destroyed by invaders from the north. Then much of the plain lapsed into sandy steppe where rainfall was too scant to sustain vegetation and dust storms plagued the herdsmen. Here copses of camel thorn are interspersed with grasslands, and willows and poplars shade the streams. Extensive pasturelands are still grazed by great herds of horses and cattle. This is the home of the small black karakul sheep from which the famous Afghan lambskin is obtained. Here too is probably the original home of the two-humped Bactrian camel, widely used in northern Afghanistan.

Some of the farmland was reclaimed in the 1930s, when new irrigation works were undertaken and some of Afghanistan's first efforts to industrialize began. Cotton and sugar beets are grown here now to supply textile and sugar factories at Baghlan, Kunduz, and Pul-i-Khumri. Coal is mined, iron ore is known to exist, and Soviet geologists search for oil.

The principal city of Afghan Turkistan is Mazar-i-Sharif, an old city that has long been famous as a Moslem pilgrimage site. Many Afghans believe that the tomb within the extensive and magnificent mosque there is that of Ali, son-in-law of the Moslem Prophet Muhammad, who founded the Shiah branch of the Moslem faith.

The Kabul River Valley

The Kabul River rises in the high mountains of central Afghanistan and, joined by its tributaries, flows 380 miles (600 kilometers) east to join the Indus River in Pakistan. Flat land along the river is well tended and fertile, but the cliffs above are bare and desolate. Fruits, grains, cotton, tobacco, and vegetables grow in irrigated fields and vineyards around both the capital city of Kabul and the smaller city of Jalalabad. The plain around Jalalabad has a climate warm enough to support citrus and palm groves.

Kabul is the largest city in the country, with a population that has probably surpassed 2 million as the result of the enormous influx of refugees displaced by guerrilla warfare. Located 6,000 feet (1,800 meters) above sea level, it is nestled in a well-sheltered plateau at the foot of bare and rocky mountains that rise abruptly on the south and west. Kabul's altitude gives it an invigorating climate, much like that of Denver, with brilliant sunlight and clear rare air. Spring is the rainy season; little rain falls during the summer. Heavy snow falls in the winter.

The contrast between the old and the new in Kabul is particularly startling. A part of the old city wall from pre-Moslem times still stands on the hills west of town, and beyond the wall is a lovely park containing the lapis-inlaid tomb of Babur, sixteenth-century founder of the Moghul Empire. On the south bank of the Kabul River stand sections of the old city, a densely packed mass of flat-roofed houses, covered bazaars, and narrow alleys.

Today many of the old bazaar areas in Kabul are being torn down to make room for broad new streets lined with shops and business houses. The guerrilla war fought between the Afghan tribesmen and the Soviets frequently intruded into these streets, as bombs and rockets exploded and assassinations marred the fabric of daily life.

The modern section of Kabul is on the flat plain north of the river. Here stand the government buildings, the foreign embassies, many schools and colleges, the few banks, and the homes of government officials and diplomatic personnel. Large tracts of new apartment houses have been built with Soviet aid.

Kabul's prominence throughout history has resulted from its location at the juncture of main routes of travel. Main roads branch out, as ancient trade routes have throughout history, in three directions. One goes north through the Salang Tunnel to Afghan Turkistan and the Amu Darya, carrying raw materials to Russia and receiving industrial equipment and military supplies from the Soviet Union. Another, extending east through the Khyber Pass to the plains of the Indian subcontinent, carries fruit and nuts to Pakistan and brings in electrical appliances, cloth, and other durable goods. A third runs south to Ghazni and Kandahar, with extensions that go on to Pakistan and the Arabian Sea and west to Herat and Iran.

The Helmand River Valley and Plain

Over the mountain divide to the south of the Kabul Valley lies the watershed of the Helmand River. The Helmand and its tributaries drain all of southern Afghanistan, an area of at least 100,000 square miles (260,000 square kilometers). To the south of the Helmand Valley, Afghanistan is bounded by the barren Baluchistan province of Pakistan. Farther west, the desolate Afghan Registan, or desert, stretches south from the Helmand River in endless shifting dunes.

The river rises near the source of the Kabul River in the central mountains of Afghanistan and flows southwest out of the mountains into a vast fertile plain. When it reaches the southern desert (Registan), it is joined by its largest tributary, the Arghandab, which waters the important urban centers of Ghazni and Kandahar. The Helmand then gradually curves westward through the desert. Near the Iranian frontier it turns abruptly north before it empties, more than 700 miles (1,100

kilometers) from its source, into a huge waste marshland, called Hamun-i
-Helmand.

The two principal cities of the Helmand Valley are capitals of provinces with the same names, Kandahar and Ghazni. Ghazni lies about
eighty miles (130 kilometers) south of Kabul at the northern end of the
Arghandab watershed, and was the capital of a magnificent empire in
the eleventh century. Old Ghazni is now in ruins, a great sweep of
mounds and rubble punctuated by two massive, lonely, and broken
minarets—all that remains today to remind one of the resplendent city
of earlier times.

Modern Ghazni is an ordinary provincial town, scenically situated on
a high ridge. Its temperate climate, which includes snowfall during the
three winter months, makes its gardens, orchards, and vineyards flour-
ish.

To the south lies Kandahar, one of the richest provinces in Afghanistan. Extremely fertile when watered, the region is famous for its
delicious fruits, melons, and grapes, and also produces large quantities
of wool. This region has traditionally traded with the subcontinent of
India. Today an excellent all-weather road runs from the city of Kandahar to the Pakistan border, where it meets a spur of the Pakistan
Railways.

The first independent monarch of modern-day Afghanistan, Ahmad
Shah, made the city of Kandahar his capital in 1747 and was buried
there. Partially surrounded by a wall, Kandahar has streets that are
wide and spacious, with open city squares. The main street is cobbled,
and the bazaars seem roomy and uncrowded in contrast to those of
Kabul. A great deal of new construction took place in the 1950s and
1960s. After the 1979 revolution, the Afghan resistance fighters succeeded repeatedly in seizing sections of the city, only to be driven out
by the superior firepower of the Afghan and Soviet armies. Much of the

farm work in the surrounding fields could be carried on only at night.

No irrigation works exist below the juncture of the Helmand and Arghandab rivers, although this vast desert area on the lower Helmand must once have supported a much larger population than it does now. In the southwest corner of Afghanistan are remains of ancient Persian cities, half buried beneath the shifting sand. In the southeast, at the junction of the Arghandab and Helmand rivers are the ruins of an eleventh-century citadel, all that remains of an important city called Bust. In the fourteenth century Turkish armies from the north massacred the population and destroyed the irrigation system of the watershed. Following their departure, centuries of hot gales and dust storms blotted out the traces of early cultivation, covering the land with endless shifting dunes.

In the 1960s extensive development projects using American construction and aid were undertaken to bring water and prosperity back to the upper Helmand and Arghandab watersheds. The Kajakai and Arghandab dams and a network of canals were designed to increase agricultural production on several thousand acres of improved and new land. Unfortunately, sufficient attention was not paid to understanding how a conservative, illiterate population would react to a new kind of agriculture. High hopes of settling large numbers of nomads were only partially realized when most of them refused to give up their wandering life. The additional agricultural capacity that the irrigation projects brought to the valley was put into production too slowly to pay for the huge investment.

The Hari Rud and Plain

The Hari Rud (the river from which Herat city and province derive their name) also rises in the high central mountains, flowing west 400 miles

(640 kilometers) across Afghanistan. After an abrupt turn northward it serves as the Afghan-Iranian border, and then passes into Soviet territory, where it fades into the desert sands. This river waters the plain of Herat in the northwest corner of Afghanistan. One of the richest districts in the country, it produces fruit and most kinds of grain, as well as silk, saffron, medicinal herbs, tobacco, nuts, and gums. Herat Province is also noted for its carpets, woolen cloth, and silk fabrics. Soviet surveys have apparently located iron and coal deposits in the area and indicated possible petroleum reserves.

The capital of Herat Province is an ancient city of the same name. Throughout history the city of Herat had been Afghanistan's main link with Iran and the Middle East. Although now shrunk in importance compared with her days of greatness, Herat remains an important trade center, sending caravans carrying hides, wool, dried fruits, and nuts to the Soviet railhead at Kushk 50 miles (80 kilometers) away.

In recent decades modern neighborhoods have grown up around the old city walls, which were constructed on a great earthwork some fifty feet (15 meters) high. The earthwork, which had five main gates leading into the city, was surrounded by a large moat. Some of the splendid Persian architectural masterpieces that graced Herat have been destroyed by fierce fighting between resistance groups and the Afghan and Soviet armies.

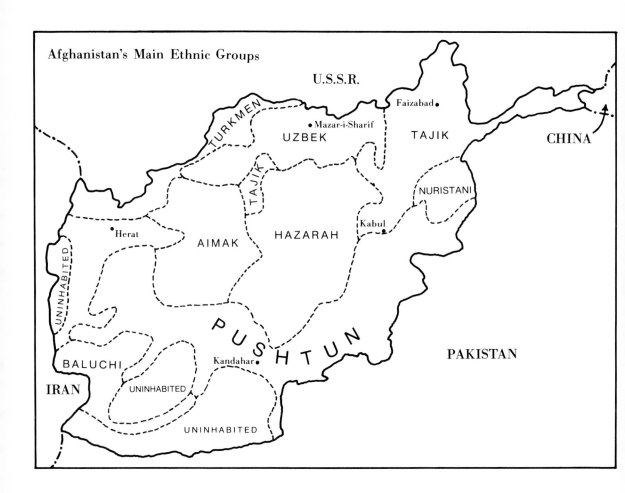

Afghanistan's Main Ethnic Groups

A Multiethnic People

Centuries of migration, invasion, and conquest have brought many different peoples to the Hindu Kush. As a result, Afghanistan has an ethnically varied population. The principal groupings are related to their neighbors in adjacent countries and share with them a long history of shifting empires. Thus the plains south of the Amu Darya are inhabited by people of Central Asian origin. The Pushtun tribes who live in the Sulayman Mountains, shared by Afghanistan and Pakistan, feel more kinship to one another than to the other ethnic groups in their own countries. The people of the Hari Rud plain not only speak Persian, but often have closer contact with Iran than with the tribes isolated from them by the mountains of the Hindu Kush.

Members of each ethnic group retain a common culture and language

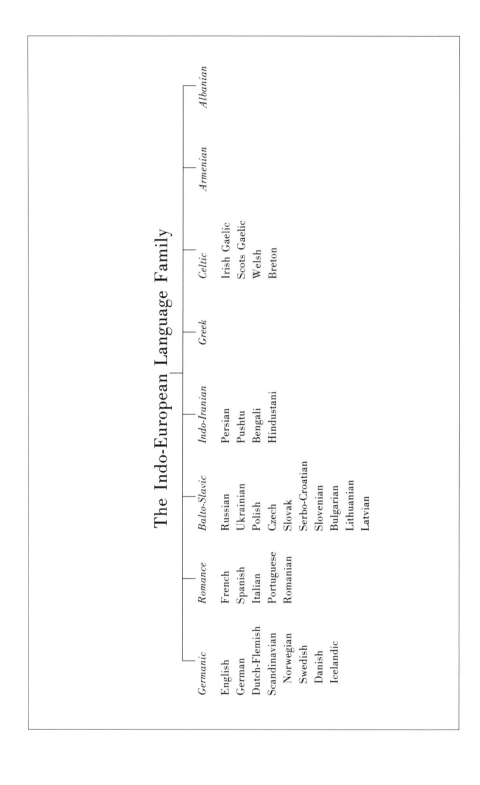

The Indo-European Language Family

Germanic	Romance	Balto-Slavic	Indo-Iranian	Greek	Celtic	Armenian	Albanian
English	French	Russian	Persian		Irish Gaelic		
German	Spanish	Ukrainian	Pushtu		Scots Gaelic		
Dutch-Flemish	Italian	Polish	Bengali		Welsh		
Scandinavian	Portuguese	Czech	Hindustani		Breton		
Norwegian	Romanian	Slovak					
Swedish		Serbo-Croatian					
Danish		Slovenian					
Icelandic		Bulgarian					
		Lithuanian					
		Latvian					

and generally enough knowledge of their traditional customs to be conscious of their ethnic identity. About twenty languages and dialects are spoken in Afghanistan. Almost all Afghans are bilingual, speaking their own dialects as well as one or both of the official languages of the country—either Dari Persian (called *Farsi* in Afghanistan) or Pushtu. Both of these languages belong to the Indo-European language family. Pushtu, the language of the Pushtuns, is spoken throughout southern and eastern Afghanistan. Persian, spoken in the western part of the country, has also predominated in the cities, and is widely used in government. Since the 1979 Soviet invasion, Russian has been taught as the compulsory foreign language in the schools.

The total population of Afghanistan is estimated to be between 15 million and 17 million—although no complete census has ever been taken. Current population estimates are based on a partial survey done by the United Nations in the 1970s. In normal times, about three quarters of the country's people are farmers, an eighth nomadic herdsmen, and the remainder urban dwellers. War has driven about one third of the population into refugee status in Pakistan and Iran.

The Pushtuns

The Pushtuns are the largest ethnic group. An estimated 7 million Pushtuns are Afghans, forming almost half the country's total population. A similar number of Pushtuns are citizens of Pakistan, living mostly in the Sulayman Range. The Pushtuns of Afghanistan occupy a huge arc extending from the mountains in the northeast down the 1,000-mile (1,600-kilometer) sweep of the Sulayman Range, across the southern Helmand Valley, and west all the way to the Iranian border and Herat.

There are several variations to their name. In India they are called

Pathans. In the northern Sulayman Range they call themselves Pukh-tuns or Pakhtuns. This book uses the softer southern variant of their name, Pushtun, and calls their language Pushtu.

This ethnic group has retained a very strong tribal identity, with a hierarchy of chiefs to maintain order and a code of honor that has shaped the outlook of the national government. Over the centuries the Pushtun men have maintained their militant heritage, loving good horses, carrying arms at all times, and exercising a degree of independence that their rulers cannot ignore. Pushtun chiefs were the first to unify the country, establishing an independent kingdom of Afghanistan. The monarchy that controlled the country until 1973 was Pushtun.

Facing Mecca, resistance fighters (mujahidin) *in Paktia Province pause for prayers while one of their number keeps watch. Paktia Province borders on Pakistan, and many fighters pass through it into Afghanistan.* Christopher Brown

They regard themselves as the "true Afghans." The Pushtun tribes figured prominently in the history of the British Empire in India and the fiction of Rudyard Kipling. Many Pushtuns were enthusiastic members of the *mujahidin* ("freedom fighters" or "holy warriors" in their own words, "rebels" in the official translation) who resisted the 1979 Soviet invasion and subsequent occupation of their country.

The Pushtuns are thought to be descendants of Aryan tribes who invaded the region of the Hindu Kush in the second millennium before Christ. The ancient Greek historian Herodotus was the first to write about the Pushtuns. In the fifth century B.C. he mentioned a people named Paktuie, living in an area that appears from his description to be the Peshawar Valley of modern-day Pakistan.

The Pushtuns themselves have a legend to explain their origin, in which they identify themselves with one of the lost tribes of Israel. According to this legend, King Saul had a grandson Afghana, who led his forty sons across the desert to the hills of Ghor (in central Afghanistan). Supposedly the Prophet Muhammad chose one of Afghana's descendants to carry Islam into Asia, and all Pushtuns can fit themselves into a remarkably consistent genealogy starting with this individual. This certainly fictional legend apparently was created after the conversion of the Afghans to Islam, when a genealogy going back to the biblical prophets whom Muhammad recognized enhanced the prestige of the Pushtuns as true Moslems.

The Pushtuns are generally tall and well built. They have light-brown skin and brown or black hair, usually brown eyes, although sometimes hazel or blue, and prominent noses. Many Pushtun men wear thick mustaches and beards and follow ancient custom by covering their heads in public with a cap or turban. The women modestly drape long scarves over their heads. Both men and women wear the Afghan national costume—long loose shirts and baggy trousers. The bandoliers of ammunition and the inevitable rifle the men sling over their shoulder give them a formidable appearance.

The Tajiks

The Tajiks are a sedentary people, numbering perhaps 3.5 million, who live in many sections of Afghanistan. They are also the principal inhabitants of the Soviet republic of Tajikistan across the northern border. They are often called *Farsiwans*, meaning "Persian-speaking." Slender and light skinned, the Tajiks have aquiline noses and usually black hair, although occasionally red or blond. Their history is vague, and it is possible that they were living in this area before the Aryan invasion.

There are several important concentrations of Tajiks in Afghanistan. The plains-dwelling Tajiks live mainly in Herat Province on the Iranian border, in Bamiyan Province, and around Kabul. They are town-dwelling traders, skilled artisans, and farmers, many of them prosperous enough to be regarded as middle class. Because they have settled in the towns, they have replaced tribal organization with village orientation and a strong sense of community loyalty. The landowners *(zamindars)* have emerged as village leaders.

Another group of Tajiks lives in the northeast mountains of Afghanistan, where they are poor, village-dwelling farmers. From their ranks emerged one of the canniest resistance leaders, Ahmad Shah Massoud, whose successes in guerrilla fighting brought repeated sweeps by the Soviets against the Tajik strongholds in the deep valleys of the northeast.

The Hazarahs

Some 1.5 million Hazarahs live in the Hazarajat, an area of rugged mountains and narrow valleys in central Afghanistan. Most of this remote countryside is extremely barren, with water very scarce. A few springs emerge from the rocky slopes, and carefully constructed channels carry every drop of unevaporated water to irrigate tiny patches of wheat. Sheep graze on the rocky slopes above.

Many Hazarahs are shepherds, following seasonal grazing lands and cultivating limited crops. They are industrious, frugal, and honest, but their terrain is too inhospitable for them to prosper. Many traditionally sought menial positions in southern and eastern Afghanistan (particularly in Kabul) to supplement their meager incomes, and were thus relegated to a low social status.

The Hazarahs are traditionally regarded as descendants of garrison troops left in the thirteenth century by the Mongol invader Genghis Khan. Although they mixed with local people, they have retained the high cheekbones, eyefolds, and sparse beards of their Mongol ancestors.

Their name comes from the Persian word *hazar*, meaning thousand, which was the size of the Mongol military unit. When Genghis Khan passed through the Hindu Kush, his destination was Persia. The followers he left behind eventually adopted the Shiah Moslem religion and the language of Persia, where a small number of their group also settled.

Military service has always appealed to the Hazarahs, and many of the young men escaped the barren central mountains by joining the army. In the 1980s this military tradition contributed to a surprisingly effective resistance to the communist government in Kabul. Some of their fervor may have stemmed from Hazarah hopes of making their region autonomous and following the example of their fundamentalist coreligionists in Iran.

The Hazarah men are clean-shaven and wear the Afghan national costume, with embroidered skullcaps instead of turbans. The women wear long dresses instead of the full trousers preferred by other rural women in Afghanistan.

The Turkish Groups of Northern Afghanistan

North of the Hindu Kush in Afghan Turkistan, a substantial number of people (perhaps 1.6 million) are descended from the Central Asian Turks who frequently invaded from the north. (These groups also spread west and gave their name to modern-day Turkey.)

The most populous Turkish group in Afghanistan is the Uzbeks (or Uzbegs), who have broad, flat faces and lighter skin than the Pushtuns. They are farmers and stockmen, breeding the karakul sheep and an excellent type of Turkman horse. These people have kinsmen in the Soviet republic of Uzbekistan. Many Uzbeks fled into northern Afghanistan in the 1920s to escape suppression when the Soviet government was trying to stamp out their customs and Moslem religion.

Less numerous are the Turkmen, who live along the southern bank of the Amu Darya, and the Kirghiz, who live in the Wakhan Corridor. Most of the Kirghiz, a nomadic people who herd yaks, were driven out of their pastures by the Soviet Army in order to stop the passage of Chinese armaments through the Wakhan Corridor.

The Turkish tribes speak an archaic form of Turkish, and generally Persian as well. The men wear large, soft leather boots, belted cloaks, and turbans. They also wear greatcoats with sleeves long enough to envelop the hands in cold weather or store away small packages. The women wear long dresses in bright floral patterns over their leggings. The nomadic tribes of Afghan Turkistan still dwell in the yurt, a dome-shaped felt tent on a collapsible wooden frame typical in Central Asia.

Other Groups

There are several other smaller ethnic groups scattered around the country, such as the Nuristanis, who live in the remote mountains northeast of Kabul along the Pakistan border. Sculptured wooden idols and ancestral images carved by the Nuristanis before they were converted to Islam in the late nineteenth century are preserved in the Kabul Museum. Some of them are almost life-size and were probably used to honor deceased ancestors and in healing ceremonies.

Half a million Chahar Aimak, whose origin is vague, live west of the Hazarajat. Baluchi nomads drive their flocks across the border from their province in Pakistan. A few small colonies of Hindu traders can be found in some of the cities.

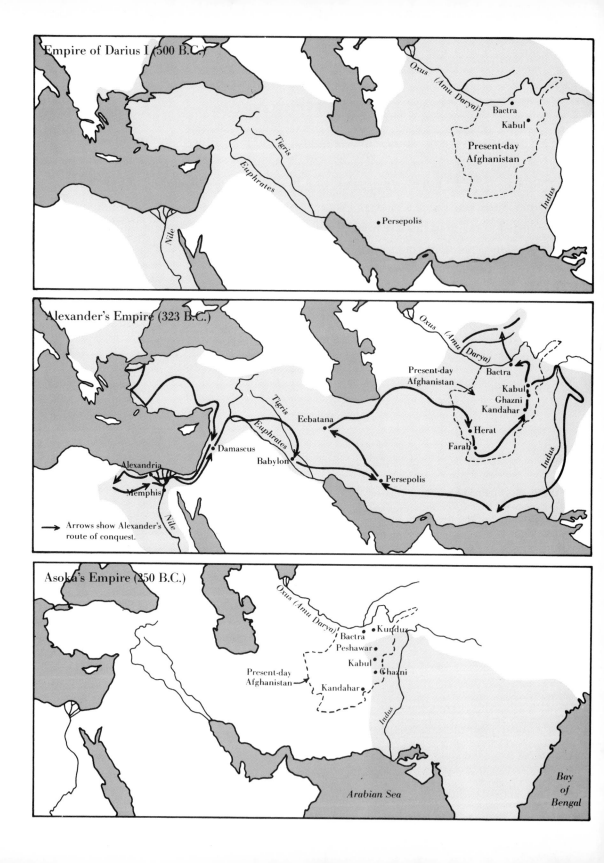

Empire of Darius I (500 B.C.)

Oxus (Amu Darya)

Tigris

Euphrates

Bactra
Kabul

Present-day
Afghanistan

Nile

Persepolis

Indus

Alexander's Empire (323 B.C.)

Oxus (Amu Darya)

Present-day
Afghanistan

Bactra

Kabul
Ghazni
Kandahar

Tigris

Ecbatana

Euphrates

Damascus

Herat

Farah

Alexandria

Babylon

Persepolis

Indus

Memphis

Nile

→ Arrows show Alexander's
route of conquest.

Asoka's Empire (250 B.C.)

Oxus (Amu Darya)

Kunduz
Bactra
Peshawar
Kabul
Ghazni

Present-day
Afghanistan

Kandahar

Indus

Arabian Sea

Bay
of
Bengal

The Beginning of History

Although Afghanistan seems to be a remote and stagnant backwater on the world stage today, known only because of its people's heroic resistance to the Soviets in the 1980s, its history sparkles with the names of some of the most important figures of Asian history.

Zoroaster

At the very beginning of its recorded history stands Zoroaster (or Zarathustra), who wrote the first known document associated with the area, the *Zend Avesta*, a sacred literary text written in Persian. Bactria, an ancient site located on the Oxus plain north of the Hindu Kush, is first mentioned in history as the probable birthplace of Zoroaster. This great religious teacher was called the "Bactrian Sage" and is believed

Outline of Afghan History

	Herat plain	Amu Darya (Oxus) plain	Kabul Valley and Upper Helmand
c. 2,000 B.C.		Ayran tribes from Central Asia move south, and eventually absorb or displace the indigenous people of the Iranian plateau and Indian subcontinent.	
600 B.C.		Zoroaster introduces a new religion in Bactria.	
540 B.C.	Persian monarch Cyrus conquers area all the way to the Jaxartes River in Central Asia, spreads Zoroaster's religion through his empire.		
500 B.C.	Under Darius the Great of Persia, all of modern Afghanistan and much of Central Asia are part of the Persian empire.		
450 B.C.			Parts of Persian empire south of the Hindu Kush break away.
331 B.C.	Alexander the Great defeats the Persian king.		
329–327 B.C.	Alexander the Great conquers all of what is today Afghanistan.		
c. 321–185 B.C.	Herat plains remain a borderland of Greek empire in Persia.	Bactria breaks away from Persian empire to become an autonomous Greek kingdom.	Native Maurya dynasty of India gains control of country south of the Hindu Kush.

	Herat plain	Amu Darya (Oxus) plain	Kabul Valley and Upper Helmand
c. 250–			Most celebrated ruler, Asoka, introduces Buddhism into Kabul River valley. Maurya empire breaking up.
184 B.C.			Bactrian Greeks conquer northern India.
c. 100 B.C.			Greek rule in Bactria disintegrates.
c. birth of Christ			Kushans of Central Asia cross the Oxus.
c. A.D. 50			Kushans cross Hindu Kush and take control of Kabul River valley (Gandhara).
c. A.D. 78–144			Most outstanding Kushan ruler, Kanishka, sponsors sculpture and art. Missionaries carry Buddhism over Great Silk Route to China and Mongolia.
c. A.D. 220			Kushan empire fragments into petty dynasties.

	Herat plain	Amu Darya (Oxus) plain	Kabul Valley and Upper Helmand
c. A.D. 224	Ardashir founds independent Sassanian dynasty in Persia. Spreads his rule to eventually include all of Afghanistan.		
c. A.D. 400		White Huns from Central Asia overrun Bactria.	
c. A.D. 420			White Huns briefly seize control of northern India.
c. A.D. 500			Indian peoples (the Mauryas) rebel and reassert control.
c. A.D. 550	Sassanian emperor reasserts control over all of what is now Afghanistan.		

to have lived in the sixth century B.C. Zoroaster was one of the first great religious figures to displace the pagan gods of his people with a monotheistic faith in a single divine creator. His doctrine was based on the unending conflict between good and evil. It also included concepts later adopted by Judaism and Christianity—free will, the immortality of the soul, and the final judgment of humanity.

Bactria was conquered by the Persian monarch Cyrus about 540 B.C. He and his successor, Darius the Great, extended their Achaemenid Empire all the way to the Jaxartes River in what is today the Soviet Union. They would be the first of many Persian kings to regard the region now known as Afghanistan as an important borderland of the Persian Empire. The religion of Zoroaster spread rapidly from its Bac-

An example of Bactrian metalwork from the 1st century B.C.   Freer Gallery of Art

trian home, becoming the principal religion of Persia until the Arab conquest of the seventh century A.D.

Zoroastrianism survives today in Iran and also among the Parsis of Pakistan and India, who fled there from Persia after the Moslem invasion. Modern trade names given to the Mazda light bulb and automobile are derived from Zoroaster's god of good, Ahura Mazda, associated with light and truth.

Persia

Between the Persian Gulf and the Caspian Sea is a high arid plateau almost surrounded by mountains, known in ancient times as Persia, today as Iran. The earliest Persians were nomads who came from the north in about 900 B.C. They were good organizers, and by 500 B.C. had built a vast empire that included most of the then-known world outside China. It boasted a relay system of mail delivery, extensive irrigation works to support agriculture, handsome cities, and the use of coins for money. Surviving ruins of the majestic palace built by Darius I and Xerxes I at Persepolis reveal the grandeur and scale of their buildings and the opulence of their courts. For centuries the Persian empire was synonymous with wealth, culture, and despotism.

In 490 B.C. the Persians invaded Greece but were driven back, ending their outward expansion. A century later Alexander the Great conquered all of Persia's vast holdings and tried to blend the Greek and Persian peoples. A Greek-Persian kingdom lasted for another hundred years before it was swept aside by new invaders, but Greek culture continued to influence the Persians.

Alexander the Great

By the middle of the fourth century B.C., the Persians were having trouble controlling the plains south and east of the Hindu Kush. In 331 B.C. a young Greek general, Alexander of Macedon, defeated the Persian armies in present-day Iraq and moved on to occupy the Persian capital. Although he destroyed Persepolis to avenge earlier Persian conquests

In A.D. 641, the Arabs brought Islam to Persia, replacing the religion of Zoroaster across much of the plateau. When the Moslem caliphs of Damascus and Baghdad ruled Persia, the country developed world-famous centers of culture and learning. Its cities were graced with beautiful mosques and palaces, and poets such as Omar Khayyam. Internal rivalries crumbled this Moslem empire after A.D. 800, and it broke up into petty kingdoms.

Seljuk Turks from Turkistan conquered much of Persia in 1037 and maintained control until they were swept away in 1221 by the hordes of Genghis Khan. His armies destroyed the great irrigation works, diminishing the land's productivity and draining away wealth and power. When the Mongol rulers began fighting among themselves in the 1400s, control of Persia passed back into the hands of a line of local kings (the Safavid dynasty). The best-known Safavid ruler, Shah Abbas I, drove back invasions by Uzbek Turks from the north and Ottoman Turks from the west. Under the Safavids the Shiah sect of Islam became predominant in Iran, rather than the mainstream Sunni doctrine. This religious division is still a great source of tension between Iran and other Moslem nations.

in Greece, Alexander was fascinated by the Persians.

Instead of treating them as a conquered people, Alexander—who had been tutored by Aristotle, the greatest thinker in the West—wanted to learn about Persian civilization and why it was so much more cultured than that of his own rocky, rural homeland. He married a Persian princess. When he learned that even more exotic lands existed beyond the empire's borders, he enlisted the Persians in his quest, appointing

the most capable among them to his staff and adding Persian legions to his army.

In 329 B.C. Alexander marched east and entered the country of the Hindu Kush, which his historians called the Paropamisus. The name survives today in one of the low western spurs of the Hindu Kush range. Afghans living in the southern plains today will tell you proudly that "Sekandar passed by here" on his march from Herat to Kandahar, a city that bears a local variant of his name. From there he moved north to the Kabul River valley and on through the Hindu Kush, where his army suffered from cold and scarce rations.

The young general spent a year conquering and garrisoning the rich lands on both side of the Oxus, advancing as far north into the Central Asian steppes as the Jaxartes River. To further encourage brotherhood among the diverse ethnic groups he gathered into his army, he married Roxana, daughter of one of the great Turkish chieftans north of the Oxus. After failing to subdue the nomadic warriors of the area, he recrossed the Hindu Kush in 327 B.C. and turned his attention to India.

The main body of his army approached India by going down the Kabul River and through the Khyber Pass. Alexander himself detoured with a small detachment up the Kunar Valley and through the northern passes to subdue hostile tribes who might harass him from the rear. The people of Nuristan today still claim descent from the ancient Greeks who garrisoned their villages.

Thus Alexander, the first of the great conquerors of the area whose deeds have been recorded for us, left the Hindu Kush. Behind him in

Many of the peoples who have passed through Afghanistan are described in the 11th-century epic poem by Firdawsi called the Shahnamah. *This illustration, from a 16th-century edition of the poem, depicts Kayumars, the legendary first ruler of Iran.* The Metropolitan Museum of Art, gift of Alexander Smith Cochran, 1913. (13.228.14, Ms.5, Fol. 4B)

Greece

The splendid civilization of ancient Greece developed on a rocky,
mountainous peninsula that juts out from southeastern Europe into
the Mediterranean Sea. In about 1500 B.C. the people of Hellas, the
Greek mainland, began building large fortified cities to shield them
from attack from the sea. Gradually the tribes around the largest
settlement in each plain and island in Greece formed an
independent community called a city-state. There was no national
government, but the Greeks shared a common culture, religion, and
language, and considered anyone whose native language was Greek
as one of them.

The following centuries saw many invasions and migrations.
Greece became overpopulated, and colonies were established on the
Black Sea, in Italy, and farther along the Mediterranean coasts.
After Persia conquered Asia Minor and became the strongest
military power in the world, the Persian emperor Darius I invaded
Greece in 490 B.C. but was decisively defeated on the Plain of
Marathon. The modern foot race of that name celebrates the 26
miles (42 kilometers) a Greek runner, Pheidippides, covered to
bring news of the great victory to Athens. The Greek states
cooperated again a few years later to repel another Persian invasion.

Thereafter, the city-state of Athens organized a defensive league
of cities and built the strongest navy in Greece. Her energies for
many decades could be devoted to sculpture, architecture,
philosophy, and drama. Some of the most important thinkers and
artists in the West, such as the philosopher Socrates, his disciple

Plato, and the tragic poets Aeschylus, Euripides, and Sophocles, lived and worked in this period. Athens fell in 404 B.C. in the Peloponnesian War. A period of decay and disintegration followed, at the same time that more primitive Macedonia to the north was steadily growing stronger. Philip II of Macedon extended his power southward until he defeated the Greeks in 338 B.C. and united them with Macedonia.

Four years later his son Alexander led an army of Macedonians and Greeks to attack the Persian Empire, and within ten years conquered everything that lay between his homeland and the Indus River in India. He founded Greek cities everywhere he went, spreading Greek culture, language, and governing structures from the Mediterranean to Central Asia.

After his death, Macedonia weakened, and many of the Greek city-states broke away to form independent leagues, the world's first attempts at representative democracy. The Romans conquered Macedonia and Greece in the first century B.C. Both became Roman provinces, but Greek culture and traditions were adopted by the Romans and lived on.

Christianity spread through Greece, particularly among the poor people. In A.D. 330 Constantine the Great moved the capital of the Roman Empire from Rome to the former Greek colony of Byzantium. Greece became part of the Byzantine Empire and enjoyed a thousand years of remarkable civilization. The Byzantine Empire finally collapsed when the Ottoman Turks captured Constantinople (formerly called Byzantium and now known as Istanbul) in 1453.

چو بهمن برادرش را کشته دید / زمین زیر خون کلاه آغشته دید
بیامد به نزدیک اسفندیار / بجایی که آتش کارزار
همی گفت کای نره شیر ژیان / سپاهی بجنگ آمد از سگزیان
دو پور تو نوش‌آذر و مهرنوش / ز بادی سگزی سپردند هوش
توانا به برد دیمانی زرد زرد / جهاندار و کی زادگان دیر کرد
ورین تخمه این ننگ تا جاودان / بماند دگر گرد تا بخردان
دل مرد بیدار شد پر ز خشم / پر از باد مغز و پر از آب چشم
ز ان خشم و کین بر گشاد او زبان / برستم چنین گفت کای بدنشان
تو گفتی که لشکر نیارم بجنگ / ز لعنت آرایش نام و ننگ
نداری ز من شرم و از کردگار / نترسی که پرسند روز شمار
ندانی که مردان پیمان شکن / ستوده نباشند در انجمن
دو سگزی دو پور مرا کشته اند / وزین خیره کین هم نه برگشته اند
چو بشنید رستم غمی گشت سخت / بلرزید برسان شاخ درخت
بجان و سر شاه سوگند خورد / بشمشیر و خورشید و دشت نبرد
که من جنگ هرگز نفرموده ام / کسی کین چنین کرد بشنوده ام
ببندم دو دست برادر کنون / که او باشد اندر بدی رهنمون
فرامرز را نیز بسته دو دست / بیارم بر شاه یزدان پرست
بکین گرانمایگان شان بکش / مشوران ازین کار بیهوده هش
چنین گفت با رستم اسفندیار / که بر کین طاوس نر خون مار
بریزم نه خوب و نه خوش بود / نه آیین شاهان سرکش بود
تو ایدر نشان چاره خویش ساز / که آمد بتنگی بمانی فراز
بر رخش باد و دمانت بتیر / بر آمیزم اکنون چو با آب شیر
بدان تا کس از بندگان زین سپس / نجویند کین خداوند بس
اگر زنده باشی ببندمت پاک / بنزدیک شاهت برم بی درنگ
وگر کشته آیی بیکان تیر / ز کین دو پور گرانمایه گیر
بدو گفت رستم کزین گفت و گوی / چه آید بجز کم شدن آبروی
بیزدان گرای و بیزدان گشای / که او هست بر نیکویی رهنمای
کمان برگرفتند و تیر خدنگ / همی کم شد از روی خورشید رنگ
ز پیکان همی آتش افروختند / بر و بر زره را همی دوختند
دل پور شاه اندران سست شد / روانها بچهرش بر آژنگ شد

هر آنکس که باشد ترا رهنمای / که بیرون شوی زین بیکی سرای
چنین گفت رستم که سوگند ... / ز رزم این زمان دست کوتاه
تو اکنون چنین از منی یاد کرد / شب تیره هرگز که جوید نبرد

رزم اسکندر با دوال پایان

من اکنون چنین سوی ایوان شوم / بیاسایم و یک زمان بغنوم
ببندم همه خستگیهای خویش / بخوانم کسی را که دارم ز پیش
زواره فرامرز و دستان سام / کسی را ز خویشان که دارند نام
بسازم کنون هرچه فرمان تست / همی با تو هم پیمان نشست
بدو گفت روئین تن اسفندیار / که ای پیر فرتوت ناسازگار
تو مردی بزرگی و زور آزمای / بسی چاره دانی و نیرنگ و رای
بدم تنت همی من فریب تو را / بخواهم که بینم نشیب تو را
بجان امشبی دادمت زینهار / بایوان شو و کام دل بر گزار
سخن هرچه بد ... ازمن مکن / وزین پس بیمای با من سخن
بدو گفت رستم که گر کنم / که بر خستگیها بر افسون کنم
چو برگشت ازو پور اسفندیار / چو بگذشت رستم خوشی در زود
ببرد آن همی داد دین داد و رود / نگه کرد تا چون رود نامدار
همی گفت ای داور دادگر / گر از خستگیها شوم من هلاک
که خواهد ز گردنکشان کین من / که گیرد دل و راه و آیین من
پس اسفندیار از پسش بنگرید / بر آن سوی رود دشت تخشکی بدید
همی گفت کین را نخوانند مرد / دگر کی نهد بیلتن بار و درد
گذر کرد با خستگیها بر آب / ازان زخم پیکان شده پر شتاب
شگفتی بماند بد اسفندیار / همی گفت کای دادگر کردگار
جهان آفرید که خود خواستی / زمان و زمین را تو آراستی
بدانگه که شد نامور با نهی / خروشیدن آمد ز پرده سرای
ز نوش‌آذر گرد و ز مهرنوش / پشوتن بیامد بر آورد جوش

Bactria he left lieutenants who would maintain a Greek colonial empire for two hundred years. He went on to subdue the Indus Valley, but at last his Macedonian soldiers demanded to return to the homeland they had left seven years earlier. Alexander led his army back to Persepolis, and died shortly thereafter (323 B.C.), ending his dreams of finding the farthest reaches of the world. The vast empire he had conquered rapidly fragmented. The generals he had left behind to administer his dominions struggled for control of Egypt and Persia. In the east the indigenous peoples of northern India were consolidated by the founder of the native Maurya dynasty, Chandragupta. He was able to gain control of both the Peshawar Valley and most of the country south of the Hindu Kush.

The Mauryas

The Mauryan Empire reached its peak in the third century B.C. under Asoka, one of the outstanding leaders in Indian history. An ardent apostle of the Buddhist religion that had developed in India around 500 B.C., Asoka established important centers of religion among the people of the Hindu Kush. Under his successors, however, his unwieldly empire gradually broke up.

Bactria, which had been part of Alexander's empire, had broken away from the Persian Empire during this period and had become an autonomous Greek kingdom. The Greeks took advantage of the breakup of the Maurya Empire and conquered northern India shortly after 200 B.C. The Bactrian Empire was soon weakened by internecine strife and pressure from nomadic tribes living in Central Asia. Within fifty years Greek sovereignty north of the Hindu Kush disappeared.

Alexander the Great fights a dragon in this 14th-century illustration of the Shahnamah. *The scene is titled "Alexander fights the Habash Monster" and was a favorite subject for miniaturists who illustrated the poem.* Museum of Fine Arts, Boston

India

From the beginning of recorded history, many people have invaded the triangular area known today as India, which lies south of the great chain of mountains that separates the Indian subcontinent from Central Asia. As early as 1500 B.C. fair-skinned people called Aryans came out of the great steppe to the north, through the mountain passes of the Hindu Kush, to become the ancestors of many present-day Indians. They found already established there the oldest living religion in the world, Hinduism, which had developed gradually over many centuries. This religion, with its reverence for all living things and its belief that man's soul must be reborn again and again until it becomes pure enough to be united with the supreme being, has been the most important influence on the culture of India.

Alexander the Great conquered the northwestern region of India in the fourth century B.C. A great indigenous empire rose after his departure, founded by Maurya and reaching its peak under the emperor Asoka. Buddhism, another of the great Eastern religions, had its origins in India in the fifth century B.C. and identified the goal of life as a state of complete release from earthly suffering and desire.

Asoka was the last ruler to unify India for over a thousand years.

Greek rule had lasted in Bactria for two centuries. Little trace remains there today, save in the folk tales of the people and in the few archeological remains, which regularly yield a profusion of ill-made

But a rich cultural life continued in the many kingdoms of the subcontinent. Music, poetry, sculpture, and dance flourished in the separate courts, and the riches of the subcontinent became legendary throughout Asia and later Europe. Control of the fabled kingdoms became the goal of many conquerors.

In 1206 came a crucial and successful invasion. Tribesmen from the western Hindu Kush established a Moslem sultanate in Delhi. The conquerors brought a new religion to the area, and Islam rose to contest with Buddhism and Hinduism for the alliegance of the Indian peoples. Religious strife is still one of the most important and divisive problems in the subcontinent.

When European traders from Portugal reached the Indian coast in 1498, they found many monarchs ruling individual Indian states. These rulers were often in fierce competition with each other for the rich trade in precious gems, ivory, and spices that Arab merchants carried from Indian ports to the Mediterranean for sale in Europe.

Babur, another Turkish Moslem, invaded from the north in 1526 and established the Moghul kingdom. His successors held brilliant court in Delhi, Agra, and Lahore until the mid-eighteenth century, when their power had so fragmented that the British gained control of much of the country. India was regarded during the nineteenth and first half of the twentieth century as the "brightest jewel in the British crown."

coins on which are recorded the profiles of the Greek rulers. The lasting influence of Greek art and culture is found farther south in the Kabul Valley, in the sculpture and art of Gandhara.

The Kushans and Gandhara

At about the beginning of the Christian era the fragmented communities of Greek Bactria succumbed to the pressure of invading nomads from the north and east. One group, the Kushans, was pushed by warring neighbors across the Oxus and occupied Bactria. Lacking any governing structure of their own, they adopted the Greek script, coinage, and administrative structure as a framework for the Kushan Empire.

In the middle of the first century A.D. the Kushans crossed the Hindu Kush and took control of the area that the Persians had called Gandhara, which extended the entire length of the Kabul River valley. Under the most celebrated Kushan ruler, Kanishka, Buddhist missionaries went forth from Gandhara along the Great Silk Route and carried Buddha's teachings into China and Mongolia. The heritage of Alexander, the Mauryas, and the Bactrian Greeks came together under the Kushans and culminated in a flowering of sculpture and art that has never been equaled since in Afghanistan.

All the famous Buddhist sites of the Hindu Kush lie adjacent to the great Buddhist pilgrimage road between India and China, particularly between the Khyber Pass and Balkh. About 150 miles (240 kilometers) northwest of Kabul is the famous valley of Bamiyan. Here, carved into a high vertical sandstone cliff, are the two largest statues of Buddha in the world—one 170 and the other 115 feet high (51 and 32 meters, respectively). Grouped around them is a long series of rock-hewn grottos that were used as monks' cells.

The daughter of an Indian ruler is married to another hero of the Shahnamah *in this early-16th-century edition of the poem.* The Metropolitan Museum of Art, gift of Alexander Smith Cochran, 1913. (13.228.16, Fol. 450b)

Persian Dominance

The Kushan dynasty ended around A.D. 220, and the indigenous people of India and Persia again asserted themselves. Early in the third century the mighty Sassanian dynasty was founded in Persia, and its rulers

Cliffs at the edge of the Bamiyan valley, into which were hewn hundreds of caves as dwellings for Buddhist monks in the 1st and 2nd centuries A.D. The tall niche contains a partially defaced statue of Buddha, 170 feet high (51 meters). United Nations

This view of the caves from a distance gives a sense of the scale of this statue of Buddha.
United Nations

dominated what are now called Transoxiana, Afghanistan, and Pakistan west of the Indus for the next four centuries. The strong Persian influence to which Afghanistan was repeatedly subjected in the centuries that followed helped shape the culture of the Afghan people.

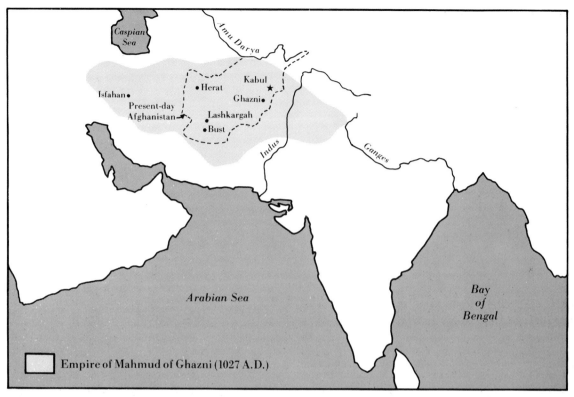

Caspian
Sea

Amu Darya

Kabul ★

Herat •

Ghazni •

Isfahan •

Present-day
Afghanistan

Lashkargah •

Bust •

Indus

Ganges

Arabian Sea

*Bay
of
Bengal*

Empire of Mahmud of Ghazni (1027 A.D.)

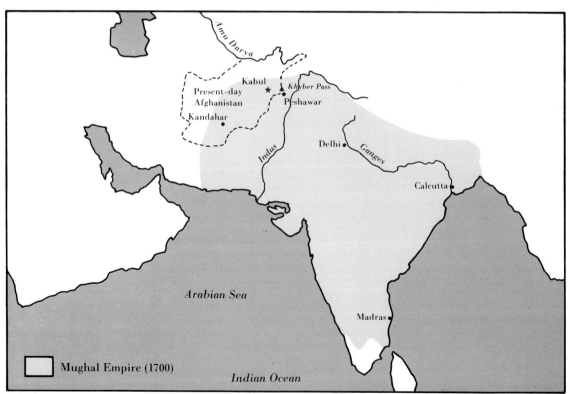

Amu Darya

Kabul ★ ▲ *Khyber Pass*

Present-day
Afghanistan

Peshawar •

Kandahar •

Indus

Delhi •

Ganges

Calcutta •

Arabian Sea

Madras •

Mughal Empire (1700)

Indian Ocean

CHAPTER V

The Banners of Islam

Arab invaders in the seventh century brought the religion of the Arab Prophet Muhammad to the peoples of the Hindu Kush. Islam's emphasis on equality, pride, and honor had immediate appeal to the sturdy mountain tribes, and in less than three hundred years the Moslem religion would be embraced by all the peoples who would someday be known as Afghans. From their midst would come important leaders who would rise to positions of power in the shifting kingdoms that competed for control of the borderlands between the Middle East, India, and Central Asia.

Outline of Afghan History

	Herat plain	Amu Darya (Oxus) plain	Kabul Valley and Upper Helmand
A.D. 652	Arab armies invade from the west.		
667	Arabs move northeast through Herat into Transoxiana.		
707–714	Arabs conquer all of Persia, invade and conquer Sind from the sea.		
c. 750	New Abbasid dynasty (Moslem) in Persia takes control of Herat plain and Transoxiana. Herat and Central Asian cities become centers of culture and learning.		
c. 800	Independent Moslem Tahirid dynasty (indigenous) seizes control.		
872			Independent Saffarid dynasty (indigenous) seizes control.
c. 900	Saffarids overthrow the Tahirids and extend Islam throughout Afghanistan.		
920		Independent Samanids from Bukhara cross the Oxus and seize control.	
962			Alptigin, a Turkish slave of the Saminids, rebels and establishes himself as ruler at Ghazni.

	Herat plain	Amu Darya (Oxus) plain	Kabul Valley and Upper Helmand
c. 980	Mahmud of Ghazni extends Ghaznavid empire from Persia to the Ganges.		
1030	After Mahmud's death, his successors compete and fragment his kingdom.		
1140			Ghorid leaders from central Afghanistan capture and burn Ghazni, then move on into India.
1220		Genghis Khan of Mongolia invades from the north, destroys cities of the north, then moves on into India through Ghazni, destroying all along his route. Turkish overlords left in charge.	
c. 1300	Hulagu, Mongol overlord of Persia, succeeds to control of Afghanistan.		
1332–1370	Descendants of earlier Ghorid rulers reassert control.		
c. 1369		Tamerlane invades from the north, ravages the Helmand Valley and conquers Northern India.	
1405	Tamerlane's fourth son, Shah Rukh, seizes Transoxiana, Herat, and eastern Iran. In his capital, Herat, a century of prosperity and the arts follows.		

	Herat plain	Amu Darya (Oxus) plain	Kabul Valley and Upper Helmand
1451			An Afghan named Buhlul seizes the throne in Delhi, founding the Lodi dynasty.
1504		Babur, son of a Timurid prince in Central Asia, loses his kingdom, moves south and takes Kabul and Ghazni.	
1526			Babur captures Delhi and founds the Moghul Empire.
1707			Moghul Empire breaks up and British gradually take control of India.
1708	Durrani Pushtuns seize control of Herat.		Ghilzai Pushtuns seize control of Kandahar.
1720	Ghilzai Pushtuns invade and seize Persia.		
1736	Nadir Quli, a Turkish tribesman from Central Asia, seizes control of Persia.		
1738			Nadir Quli captures Kabul and Delhi.
1747	Nadir Quli assassinated. Pushtuns under Ahmad Shah capture Kandahar and found modern kingdom of Afghanistan.		

The Arab Invasion

The new religion, which had been adopted throughout the Arabian Peninsula in the seventh century, was rapidly spread by zealous Moslem armies mounted on swift horses both westward to the Atlantic and eastward across Persia and Central Asia to the borders of the Chinese Empire. After the invading Arab armies had conquered the Sassanid Empire in Persia, an Arab expedition in 652 pushed on into the flat southern plains of what is today Afghanistan, there encountering rugged tribesmen whom they called "Avghans" or "Afghans"—the first time the name is recorded in history. The term meant "horseman" or "cavalier."

In 667 the Arabs moved through Herat province and the northern plains to cross the Oxus. It took another fifty years for them to establish a firm hold on the Turkish tribes who lived on the plains north of the Oxus and to reach the Indus River in the south. During these years Islam was widely accepted in the chief centers of Afghanistan and Central Asia, but the inhabitants of the less accessible ranges of the Hindu Kush were not converted until a later date.

A New Persian Dynasty

In the middle of the eighth century a dynasty of Persian Moslems, the Abbasids, ruled the Iranian plateau and won over the entire Turkish population of Transoxiana. In Baghdad under the famous Caliphs Harun-al-Rashid and his son Mamun, the arts and sciences flourished and *The Thousand and One Nights* was added to the world's folk literature. Merv, Balkh, and Samarkand in Central Asia became important outposts for the studying and teaching of Islam.

In the ninth century the Abbasids' power waned, and in Afghanistan three short-lived local kingdoms supplanted the Persians. One of these, the first of Afghan stock to arise after the Arab conquest, was the first to unite the regions both north and south of the Hindu Kush under one rule. In this period Islam was extended among the more remote Afghan tribes and the use of the Dari language of Persia encouraged.

By 920 Samanid Turks of Central Asia had established their headquarters in Bukhara north of the Oxus and extended their control from the borders of India to the neighborhood of Baghdad. Within a generation this dynasty began to decay, its kings falling under the influence of enslaved Turkish war prisoners who fought for control of military factions. One of these, Alptigin, established himself as an independent ruler at Ghazni in 962. He founded the Ghaznavid dynasty, and during the next hundred years the plains around Ghazni were dotted with palaces, mosques, monuments, and tombs, and all the famous men of the time congregated in the capital.

The Ghaznavids

Mahmud of Ghazni, the third and greatest of the Ghaznavid line, extended the empire to include the greater part of Persia in the west, and in the east India to the Ganges. Through a series of seventeen expeditions Mahmud extinguished Hindu power west of the Indus and set up the standard of Islam to rally the Afghan tribes to his army. Although he himself was a Turk, his armies were largely composed of Afghan tribesmen, mercenaries who formed the spearhead of the Moslem invasion of India.

This was the period of the final conversion of the Afghans to Islam, the period of their emergence from their remote mountains into the full light of history. They rose to the top in the land of their conquest, to the throne of Delhi, and to other important commands. They were prominent in India for the next three hundred years: Even the Moghul emperors depended on them for military strength.

With the wealth obtained from the rich cities of India, Mahmud beautified and expanded Ghazni and endowed universities and seats of learning. Famous scholars attended his court. The poet Unsari was among them, as was the scientist and historian al-Biruni. Most illustrious of all was the poet Firdawsi, who was entrusted by the monarch with the task of writing the *Shahnamah,* or *Book of Kings*, an epic of 60,000 rhyming couplets that tells the saga of four Persian dynasties.

Most of the tremendous monuments built by Mahmud and his son Masud have long since disintegrated or been destroyed, but the magnificent tomb that Masud erected for his father in a small village a little over a mile (a kilometer and a half) northeast of Ghazni still remains, as do two minarets along the road. These towers, star shaped in plan and decorated with brickwork, are nearly 100 feet (30 meters) high without their lost crowning features, and probably marked the corners of a mosque that was 1,300 feet (400 meters) long on each side. Bronze receptacles, ceramic bowls, and similar artifacts also remind us of a city noted for its university, talented teachers, learned men, and famous poets.

At the juncture of the Helmand and Arghandab rivers is the site of Bust, today known as Kalah Bust. Bust was already a great city at the time of the Arab conquest. The ruins on the site today spread over dozens of acres and are of a colossal Ghaznavid citadel, the interior of which is filled with centuries of drifted sand. Like most of Afghanistan's ancient sites, excavation has barely begun, but several decades ago archeologists opened up an impressive circular shaft several stories deep, which reveals only a small portion of what may lie buried there. At the foot of the citadel walls stands a splendid arch of fired brick decorated with bright patterns of the same material, which was restored

Selection praising Shah Mahmud of Ghazni, from the *Shahnamah* of the poet Firdawsi, completed in 1010 at Mahmud's court. The poem covers Persian history from the creation through almost four thousand years of mythical and historical reigns, and took Firdawsi thirty-five years to complete.

> God bless the Shah, the pride of crown and throne
> And signet-ring, bless him whose treasuries groan
> With his munificence, what while the fame
> Of majesty is heightened by his name.
> From sea to sea hosts answer to his call,
> The Glory of his crown is over all;
> No gold is in the mine, to men unknown,
> That fortune hath not reckoned as his own;
> And, God assisting him to all his ends,
> He spoileth foemen to enrich his friends.
> At feast he scatters treasure, while in fight
> The elephant and lion feel his might.
> And when he dominates lands in war
> He brings doomsday with his scimitar;
> But, whether jewels with his hand he fling,

by the Afghan government.

A few miles north of Bust near the modern town of Lashkargah are the extensive remains of a winter residence and military camp of the Ghaznavid rulers. When snows lay on the hills of Ghazni, the court moved to three fortified mud-brick palaces in this warmer spot beside the Helmand River. The outlines of the rooms are still marked by the crumbling walls, with door and window openings looking out over the river. Latrines, bathrooms for the apartments, and a duct for running

Or wield a sword, he seeks one sole thing—
That heaven at feast shall hail him as a sea,
In fight as sun-faced lion. All agree—
Earth, water, and the heavenly Fount of light—
That such another Shah ne'er was for fight,
For gifts and toil, for glory and renown.
Mixed he not love with war he would bring down,
When wroth, the stars. Strong is he, his array
Such that therein the wind is barred of way.
Seven hundred elephants of mighty size
Bring up his army's rear, and his allies
Are God and Gabriel. From all the great
He claims tribute, and from every state;
While, if they pay not, all is lost to them—
Their country, treasure, throne, and diadem.
Who dare break fealty with him or slight
His bidding who at feast is this world's light,
And mountain with the breastplate on in fight?

From *The Shahnama of Firdausi,* translated into English by Arthur George
Warner and Edmond Warner (London: Kegan Paul, Trench, Trubner and Co.,
Ltd., 1905)

water that supplied three pools in the reception rooms indicate that the
rulers enjoyed considerable luxury and comfort in the eleventh century.
To the east of the palaces are extensive walled areas that were once
gardens, courtyards, and other buildings.

Mahmud died in 1030. His empire, like many that depend on a great
military genius, declined after his death. About a dozen Ghaznavid
rulers fought among themselves for the next 125 years. During this
period tribes from the central mountains of Ghor began to raid their

A nineteenth-century drawing of the tomb of Mahmud of Ghazni. Nancy Hatch Dupree, *Afghanistan,* Oxford: S. Gupta, 1972.

neighbors. The Ghaznavid Empire crumbled and eventually fell to a Ghorid dynasty that survived for a short time in the heights of the western Hindu Kush.

In 1140 the Ghorids captured and burned to the ground the magnificent city of Ghazni, and went on to conquer India. Their followers, Turko-Afghan tribesmen, focused so much of their attention on India that they almost forgot their mountain homeland. One of the Ghorid

An old photograph of the minaret of Masud at Ghazni. The caps are no longer in place on top of the columns. Jeannine Auboyer, *The Art of Afghanistan,* Hamlyn House: Feltham, Middlesex, England, 1968

Turkistan

North of the high mountain range that separates the Indian subcontinent from Central Asia lies a vast sweep of grassland generally called steppe. Treeless and with very limited rainfall, the steppe in ancient times supported only a very scattered population of nomadic herdsmen who took great pride in their horses and their ability to fight. In the east lived an ethnic group called Mongols, in the center and west were Turks, descendants of a Mongol tribe called Huns who in the fifth century conquered the rich trading cities of Bukhara and Samarkand on the Great Silk Route and invaded the Roman Empire. The homeland of these Turkish tribes in Central Asia was often called Turkistan.

Periodically, a great leader—Attila was the first—would show a special aptitude for military organization and weld a group of tribes together into a fighting force that could subject their neighbors. Fierce, mobile, and relentless, they were the terror of Asia and Europe. The Seljuk Turks, for example, moved west in the eleventh century into Asia Minor and displaced the Byzantine emperors of Constantinople. Two centuries later Ottoman Turks also moved west and established an empire that was the forerunner of modern Turkey.

While the Seljuk Turks were moving west, Mongolian tribes were

generals, Kutb-ud-din, who had been a Turkish slave of the Ghorids, gained the throne in Delhi and was followed for nearly a century by a succession of Turkish slave kings who were supported by Afghan tribesmen.

consolidating an empire at the eastern end of the steppe. The most famous of the Mongol leaders was Genghis Khan, who led his horsemen out of far Mongolia in the thirteenth century to sweep across the Central Asian plains all the way to the gates of Europe. The huge empire he established was too unwieldy to maintain intact, and struggles among his successors split it into sections.

In the fourteenth century another strong leader arose in the heart of Turkistan. Tamerlane unified the Turkish tribes around his birthplace, Samarkand, and set out west and south to conquer India and the Middle East. His empire, too, disintegrated after his death.

Without strong leadership, the tribes fragmented, each grazing its traditional grasslands and maintaining an uneasy peace with its neighbors when forage was adequate. When droughts forced them farther afield to seek food for their animals, fighting over water sources and pastureland inevitably resulted.

In the fifteenth century Russian rulers to the north began to expand their territories east into Siberia and south into Turkistan. Most of western Turkistan came under Russian control during wars against the Ottoman Empire in the 1800s. The czar's government created a province called Turkistan, with its capital at Tashkent. In the 1920s the new U.S.S.R. government divided Turkistan into five Soviet republics, each named for the predominant ethnic group living there.

The only monument left to recall the sultans of Ghor is a tall, fragile minaret standing completely alone by a stream in an empty valley in the remote ranges of Ghor province. It was perhaps the center of the Ghorid capital, completely destroyed by the Mongols in 1222. Twenty-

six feet (eight meters) wide at the base and 200 feet (60 meters) high, the minaret is completely decorated with geometric panels composed of fragments of brick set in a bed of plaster, interspersed with bands of Kufic inscription that reproduce a chapter of the Koran.

The Mongol Invasion

The next tide of invasion came from the northeast, out of distant Asia, and brought only destruction to the people of the Hindu Kush. In the thirteenth century the Mongol chieftan Genghis Khan united his people into a disciplined fighting force. Fired with his success in seizing control of Mongolia, Genghis Khan aspired to conquer the world. Mounted on small, fleet ponies, the Mongols poured forth from their remote fast-nesses and swept like a hurricane over the vast steppes and mountain ranges, mercilessly destroying as they passed the cities and centers of commerce, the religious shrines and monuments of civilization, the fields of grain and irrigation systems, the very population—until the land they passed over lay waste and desolate.

In 1220 Genghis Khan reached the Oxus. When the unfortified city of Balkh surrendered, he ordered the massacre of all its inhabitants and the destruction of the entire city with its numerous mosques, schools, and other public buildings. Herat met the same fate.

The following year the Mongols crossed the Hindu Kush. There Genghis besieged and destroyed the old Buddhist city in the Bamiyan Valley. After ravaging the countryside all the way to the banks of the Indus, the hordes turned back from the approaching hot weather of the Indian plains. Ordering his lieutenants to destroy Ghazni to prevent its

The court of the Turks looks on as a hero, Siawush, displays his skill in hunting. This illustration of the Shahnamah *was drawn in the middle of the 17th century.* The Metropolitan Museum of Art, gift of Alexander Smith Cochran, 1913. (13.228.17, Fol. 100a)

use as a base by any local leaders, Genghis marched north to Peshawar, which he destroyed, and by 1223 was once more across the Oxus.

Behind him he left ruin. The population was devastated. The great cities were reduced to vast expanses of rubble. The desert winds blew sand over them and over the once-plowed fields, filling in the irrigation ditches and wells. For the next hundred years the country lay prostrate under the Mongol grip. The local rulers were usually Turks who administered the country on behalf of their Mongol overlords. Genghis Khan was succeeded by his son Ogatai, and then as the Mongol Empire fragmented, the Afghan tribes fell under the rule of Hulagu, founder of a Mongol dynasty in Persia. By the middle of the fourteenth century the Mongol hold was relaxing, and the country was divided into a number of small principalities ruled by Turkish chieftains. The traces of Mongol rule gradually disappeared, save in the bleakness of the countryside they had overrun and in the marked resemblance of the Hazarah people who live in the central mountains of Afghanistan to their Mongol ancestors.

Two famous travelers passed through the mountain crossroads in this period and left extensive records of their impressions. Between 1271 and 1275 Marco Polo was en route from the Mediterranean to the Peking court of Kublai Khan, Genghis's grandson who had inherited Mongol authority in China. Marco Polo traveled overland along the Great Silk Route, the ancient trade route of Central Asia that passed through Balkh and Badakhshan. Many of the things he mentioned in his record of his travels are still typical in that area today—"the best melons in the world," "fruit, corn [grain], and vines," "almond and pistachio nuts," "good wheat," "oil . . . from certain nuts, and from the grain called sesame," "innumerable quantity of sheep," and horses that "are of a superior quality and have great speed."

Marco Polo recorded the destruction of Balkh. The people of the area he described as "Mahometans," "blood-thirsty and treacherous," "keen sportsmen," "expert at the chase." He believed the people of "Bala-shan" [Badakhshan] when they told him their rulers were "all descended from Alexander."

Another famous chronicle of the area was written in 1333 by a traveler from Moslem North Africa, a Moor of mixed Arab and Berber descent, Ibn Battuta. "We crossed the Oxus . . . and after a day and a half's march through a sandy waste reached Balkh. It is an utter ruin and uninhabited. . . . The accursed Tinkiz [Genghis Khan] destroyed this city. . . ." He speaks of Herat as "the largest inhabited city in Khurasan." Ibn Battuta gives an interesting explanation of the name of the Hindu Kush, which means "Slayer of Hindus": "The slave boys and girls who are brought from India die there in large numbers as a result of the extreme cold and the quantity of snow."

He visited Kabul—"formerly a vast town, the site of which is now occupied by a village inhabited by a tribe of Persians called Afghans." They "hold mountains and defiles and possess considerable strength, and are mostly highwaymen. Their principal mountain is called Kuh Sulayman." Of Ghazni he wrote that "the greater part of the town is in ruins . . . though it was once a large city." His journey from Ghazni into India apparently met with some interference from Afghan mountain tribes.

Tamerlane

The relaxation of Mongol control in the fourteenth century permitted descendants of the Ghorids in Herat to attain virtual independence between 1332 and 1370. By the end of this time, however, Timur-i-Lang (Tamerlane), a Moslem descendant through his mother from Genghis Khan, had led Turkish hordes from his capital, Samarkand, to establish another empire that included the Afghans. On several occasions he crossed the Hindu Kush, the most famous in 1398 when he invaded India and ravaged Delhi, leaving in his wake another trail of destruction. Much of the country of the Hindu Kush met a similar fate at his hands—particularly evident today in the dry wastes of the Helmand Valley.

Timur was not as completely destructive as his Mongol predecessors, however, and his descendants brought an era of progress and prosperity to some areas. Timur himself encouraged the arts and enriched his capital, Samarkand, with magnificent buildings, some of which still stand in the modern city in the Uzbek Republic of the U.S.S.R. In other parts of his empire he constructed important public works and reorganized administration. He encouraged commerce and industry, opening up new trade routes, especially between his homeland and India.

At the time of Timur's death in 1405 his fourth son, Shah Rukh, triumphed in a family feud for power and secured control of Herat, eastern Iran, and the plains north of the Hindu Kush. He rebuilt the walls of his capital, Herat, and adorned it with magnificent buildings. Beautiful Moslem architecture from the fifteenth century can still be seen in the *madrasa* (college) attached to the much older great mosque (begun in 1200). Herat became the political and commercial metropolis of the area. Architects, painters, scholars, and musicians were held in high esteem.

In the fifteenth century Herat became the center of Persian miniature painting, originally created for the illustration of writings of the rulers, historians, and poets. The greatest of all the Persian miniature painters, Kamal-ud-din Bihzad, was born in Herat in about 1440 and lived at the court of the last of the great Timurid princes.

North of the Hindu Kush, the most revered mosque in Afghanistan was constructed in Mazar-i-Sharif. Its portals, towers, minarets, and domes are sumptuously decorated with glazed mosaics in which cobalt blue and turquoise predominate. Sparkling in the sun, this monument is still Afghanistan's most beautiful example of Moslem architecture.

The Timurid dynasty in Afghanistan lasted for a century, but then the empire gradually decayed. As the power of foreign masters dwindled, the indigenous people again revitalized and exerted themselves. Several local chieftains established their rule over different parts of the area. One of the most noted of them was an Afghan, Buhlul Lodi. In 1451 Buhlul seized the throne at Delhi and founded the Lodi dynasty, which lasted there for seventy-five years. The Afghans as a people shared his royal prestige, and scores of them moved down from the highlands of the Hindu Kush into the frontier hills and the plains of India, where they were eventually absorbed into the local population.

The Moghul Empire

As the sixteenth century began, a Moslem chief from Central Asia invaded the Indian subcontinent and established an empire that lasted until the British finally took control 250 years later. The Afghan tribes played an important part both in forging the military power of the Moghul Empire and in its final disintegration.

Zahir-ud-din Muhammad Babur, the eldest son of a Timurid prince from Central Asia, was a Turk and a Moslem, as his great-great-great-grandfather Tamerlane had been, and he claimed descent through his mother from Genghis Khan. The Indians called Babur and his successors "Moghuls," a word for Mongol, because he aspired to regain the glory of the Mongol Empire of Genghis Khan.

Babur lost his homeland to the Turkish Uzbeks. In 1504, defeated and almost destitute, he set out with a few hundred followers for Balkh, took Kabul and Ghazni, and in 1505 proclaimed himself heir to the

Excerpt from the *Memoirs of Zahir-ud-Din Muhammed Babur, Emperor of Hindustan* in the Chaghatai Turki. The year is 1504.

The people of Hindustan [land of the Hindus; India] call every country beyond their own Khorasan, in the same manner as the Arabs term all except Arabia, Ajem. On the road between Hindustan and Khorasan, there are two great marts: the one Kabul, the other Kandahar. Caravans, from Ferghana, Turkistan, Samarkand, Balkh, Bukhara, Hissar, and Badakhshan, all resort to Kabul; while those from Khorasan repair to Kandahar. This country lies between Hindustan and Khorasan. It is an excellent and profitable market for commodities. Were the merchants to carry their goods as far as Khita [northern China] or Rum [Turkey], they would scarcely get the same profit on them. Every year, seven, eight, or ten thousand horses arrive in Kabul. From Hindustan, every year, fifteen or twenty thousand pieces of cloth are brought by caravans. The commodities of Hindustan are slaves, white clothes, sugar-candy, refined and common sugar, drugs, and spices. There are many merchants that are not satisfied with getting thirty

empire of Tamerlane. He made Kabul his capital, both because of its strategic and economic importance and because he found its scenery and climate delightful. His memoirs frequently refer to that city. Although he never returned there after his conquest of northern India, he was buried there by his own request under the great chenar trees in a garden he planted. The Afghans still visit his tomb and remember him with admiration.

Babur spent twenty years trying to gain control of the Afghan tribes of the Sulayman Range and Kandahar, endeavoring to consolidate a or forty for ten. The productions of Khorasan, Rum, Irak, and Chin [China], may all be found in Kabul, which is the very emporium of Hindustan. Its warm and cold districts are close by each other. From Kabul you may in a single day go to a place where snow never falls, and in the space of two astronomical hours, you may reach a spot where snow lies always, except now and then when the summer happens to be peculiarly hot. In the districts dependent on Kabul, there is great abundance of fruits both of hot and cold climates, and they are found in its immediate vicinity. The fruits of the cold district in Kabul are grapes, pomegranates, apricots, peaches, pears, apples, quinces, jujubes [resemble a plum], damsons, almonds, and walnuts; all of which are found in great abundance. I caused the sour-cherry tree to be brought here and planted; it produced excellent fruit, and continues thriving. The fruits it possesses peculiar to a warm climate are the orange, citron, the amluk [lotus], and sugar-cane. . . ."

Translated by John Leyden and William Erskine (London: Humphrey Milford, Oxford University Press, 1921), Volume I, pp. 219–220.

firm base for operations into India. He invaded the subcontinent at the head of a Turko-Afghan army and in 1526 captured Delhi from its Lodi Afghan sultan. The remaining four years of Babur's life were spent in consolidating his widespread dominions.

The fortunes of the new dynasty remained doubtful for the next twenty years, and not until Babur's grandson Akbar mounted the throne was the Moghul Empire finally secure. The country of the Hindu Kush became an outpost, guarding the approaches to its northern and western frontiers.

The Afghan tribes of the Sulayman Range, who speak Pushtu rather than Persian and are called Pushtuns, played an important part in the history of these years. The Moghul armies drew heavily on them for recruits. On the other hand, these Pushtun warriors clung fiercely to their independence in their own mountains. During the reign of the Emperor Shah Jahan, famous for building the Taj Mahal in India, a renowned fighter who became known as the Afghan Warrior Poet lived in the rugged foothills of the Hindu Kush. Khushal Khan Khattak (1613–1690) was a leader in the fight of the Afghan tribes against Moghul domination. His poems, which echo the popular tribal tales of heroism, battle, and victory, are responsible for his lasting place in the memory of his people.

Khushal Khattak served in several Moghul campaigns, and was named guardian of the king's highway to Peshawar. The next Moghul emperor, Aurangzeb, reduced Khushal Khattak's position, however, and had him imprisoned for two years. Aurangzeb's reign was marred by a great rebellion of the Pushtun tribes around the Khyber Pass. Khushal Khattak was a hostage of the Moghul troops who tried to quell this revolt. By this time he had the deepest contempt for Aurangzeb and spent the rest of his life in open rebellion against the Moghuls, attempting to unite his tempestuous tribesmen against them. The revolt was finally put down and the area kept quiet by a series of strong governors and the payment of subsidies to the tribes.

The fabric of the Moghul Empire had been undermined by Aurangzeb's mismanagement, and rapidly fell to pieces after his death in 1707. This disintegration of Moghul rule was one of the principal reasons for British expansion in India. The British East India Company, founded in 1600 and based in Calcutta, found that Indian wars and politics interfered with its trading operations. To protect their trade the British gradually extended their control farther and farther into northern India.

Khushal Khan Khattak wrote in the Pushtu language in the seventeenth century during the reign of the Moghul emperors. The following stanza, referring to the destructiveness of tribal rivalries, mentions several Pushtun (Pathan) tribes—the Mohmunds, the Bangash, the Warrakzais, and the Afridis—who live in the Sulayman Mountains (land of Roh).

Of the Pathans that are famed in the land of Roh,
Now-a-days are the Mohmunds, the Bangash, and the Warrakzais,
    and the Afridis.
The dogs of the Mohmunds are better than the Bangash,
Though the Mohmunds themselves are a thousand times worse than the dogs.
The Warrakzais are the scavengers of the Afridis,
Though the Afridis, one and all, are but scavengers themselves.
This is the truth of the best of the dwellers in the land of the Pathans,
Of those worse than these who would say that they were men?
No good qualities are there in the Pathans that are now living:
All that were of any worth are imprisoned in the grave.
This indeed is apparent to all who know them.
He of whom the Moghuls say, "He is loyal to us,"
God forbid the shame of such should be concealed!
Let the Pathans drive all thought of honour from their hearts:
For these are ensnared by the baits the Moghuls have put before them.

From C. Biddulph, *Afghan Poetry of the 17th Century: Being Selections from the Poems of Khushul Khan Khatak* (London, 1890)

Reemergence of Afghan Leadership

The Afghans had played a role in the disintegration of the Moghul Empire. In the two hundred years that the Moghuls had ruled from Delhi, the border cities of the Hindu Kush were the focus of a three-sided struggle between the Moghuls, the Persians in the west, and the Turkish Uzbeks in the north. Kabul, Herat, and Kandahar changed hands again and again. In Kandahar the frequent shifts from Persian to Moghul suzerainty and back again encouraged the powerful local tribes to play one power against the other.

In 1708 one tribe of Pushtuns overthrew Persian control of Kandahar, while at Herat another tribe of Pushtuns followed suit. Within a few years these tribes had taken control of a large part of the Persian Empire. They overextended themselves, however, and their Persian rule soon disintegrated. Their small armed force lacked adequate support from their homeland to sustain them. Jealousies and intrigues among their leaders soon led them to lose not only Persia, but Kandahar itself.

A Turkish tribesman named Nadir Quli Khan (later known as Nadir Shah of Persia) broke the Pushtun power and rallied Persia to his leadership. Many Pushtun chiefs fled to Kabul, which gave Nadir Quli an excuse to capture it in 1738. He moved on to plunder the fabulous Moghul treasures of Delhi, including the Peacock Throne and the Koh-i-nur diamond, which he carried off to his capital, Meshed.

Among Nadir Quli's officers was a Pushtun chief, Ahmad Khan Sadozai. He rose to be the trusted commander of Nadir Quli's Afghan bodyguard. In 1747, Nadir Quli was assassinated by his Persian officers. Ahmad Khan with a strong contingent of Pushtun troops fought his way out of the Persian camp, seized a treasure convoy, and marched to Kandahar. There he had himself elected Amir, paramount chief of his tribe, and set about consolidating an empire.

In the centuries that followed, Afghanistan was invaded again, but 1747 marks the end of the period during which the country we know today passed in and out of neighboring empires. The region north of the Oxus passed into the control of czarist Russia. To the east the

British consolidated their control in India. And in the west Britain guaranteed the integrity of Persia's borders. With the rise of Ahmad Khan Sadozai, the area between the three became a new state in Central Asia.

The Royal Government of Afghanistan

From 1747 until 1973, when its form of government was changed to a republic, the independent kingdom of Afghanistan was ruled by important members of the Pushtun ethnic group, the most militant among the Afghans, whose ancestral home is in the Sulayman Mountains that straddle the country's eastern border. These Pushtun rulers were largely preoccupied on the one hand with wooing or subjecting both the rival Pushtun tribes and the many other ethnic groups that were gathered into their kingdom and, on the other hand, with countering the encroachment of two great powers, Great Britain and Russia, against their borderlands.

Genealogical Table of the Sadozai Family
(which provided rulers of Afghanistan from 1747 to 1826/dates show years of rule)

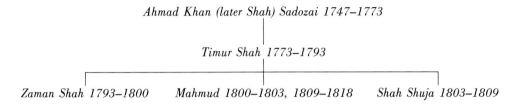

Ahmad Khan (later Shah) Sadozai 1747–1773

Timur Shah 1773–1793

Zaman Shah 1793–1800   *Mahmud 1800–1803, 1809–1818*   *Shah Shuja 1803–1809*

1818–1826 Timur Shah's many sons struggle for the throne

Ahmad Shah Durrani

In 1747 the new leader of the Afghans changed his title from khan (chief) to shah (king in Persian) and assumed the name Durrani (Pearl of Pearls). Immediately he began to consolidate and enlarge his kingdom. He seized Kabul. He wrested from the Moghuls their territories west of the Indus. He besieged Herat in the west and gained control of the plains in the north as far as the Oxus. In 1756 he occupied Delhi and carried off as much wealth as possible, thereby enriching his treasury. By 1761 his empire was much larger than present-day Afghanistan.

Ahmad Shah was an outstanding general and a just ruler. He governed with the help of a council of chiefs, each responsible for his own people. Thus all matters of national importance were centralized, but each chief ruled his own tribe, provided contingents for defense, and received payments for such services. This arrangement embodied the tribal pattern of the chieftan as first among his equals, won the support of the people, and was the prevailing political pattern in Afghanistan until the monarchy ended in 1973.

Ahmad Shah's vast realm soon broke apart. Afghans were better fighters than administrators. In the forty-five years following Ahmad Shah's death in 1773, prolonged jealousies and feuds among rival claimants to the throne led to the disintegration of the ruling family, and very nearly to the total dismemberment of Afghanistan.

Ahmad Shah's second son and heir, Timur Shah, moved his capital from Kandahar to Kabul, and ruled for twenty years over an extensive but insecure empire. He left twenty-three sons, but failed to nominate an heir. During the next quarter century the royal princes plotted and intrigued for possession of the Afghan throne while their empire fell apart around them. Three different brothers briefly secured the throne, one of them twice, each soon falling victim to the family intrigues. Their treachery was not confined to one another, but extended to their loyal supporters and advisers. After Shah Shuja had executed an important subsidiary chieftan and blinded his eldest son, the Muhammadzai clan rose in rage. In 1818 the youngest of the Muhammadzai sons, Dost Muhammad, challenged and defeated Shah Mahmud of the Sadozai family near Kabul.

Dost Muhammad

Although the Muhammadzais continued to acknowledge the nominal overlordship of the Sadozai shahs, there was little left of the great kingdom of Ahmad Shah. In the north Balkh had asserted its independence, while provinces across the Oxus had been taken by czarist Russia. To the east the Sikhs, members of a monotheistic religious community, a synthesis of Hinduism and Islam founded in the fifteenth century, controlled the northern Indus Valley, while the British moved into the south. In the west the refugee Sadozai princes of the previous ruling family established themselves in Herat, while Dost Muhammad's

Genealogical Table of the Barotzai Family (Muhammadzai Clan)

(which provided rulers of Afghanistan from 1834 to 1973/dates show years of rule)

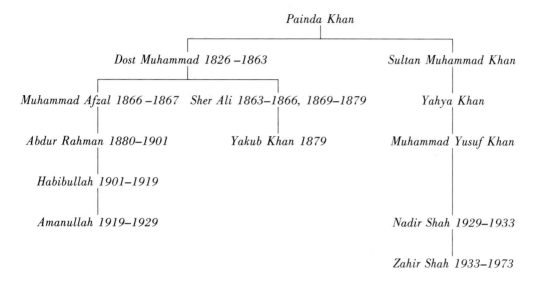

Painda Khan

Dost Muhammad 1826–1863　　　　　*Sultan Muhammad Khan*

Muhammad Afzal 1866–1867　*Sher Ali 1863–1866, 1869–1879*　　*Yahya Khan*

Abdur Rahman 1880–1901　　　*Yakub Khan 1879*　　　*Muhammad Yusuf Khan*

Habibullah 1901–1919

Amanullah 1919–1929　　　　　　　　　　　*Nadir Shah 1929–1933*

Zahir Shah 1933–1973

older brothers took control of the provinces south of Ghazni.

Dost Muhammad took control of Kabul in 1826 and had no sooner proclaimed himself Amir of Afghanistan in 1835 when the Sikhs began to expand their claim to the Peshawar area. Since the Sikhs were tacitly supported by the British, Dost Muhammad asked the British governor general of India to intervene. In return, he implied that the Afghans could bolster the northwestern approaches to British India against the Russians. Dost Muhammad had come to the Afghan throne at the time the two great empires were expanding: The British in India were moving north, the Russians in Central Asia moving south. Eventually only the land of the Hindu Kush remained between them. Afghanistan was caught in the great powers' struggle in the nineteenth century—and eventually became a buffer state between them.

When Dost Muhammad made his request for help against the Sikhs, the British were not ready to trust the Afghans. The memory of the last great Afghan invasion of India under Ahmad Shah was still fresh enough to suggest that these fierce neighbors on the mountain crossroads might be a threat to British rule in India. In fact, within two years the British were to force Dost Muhammad off his throne.

When Dost Muhammad asked the British for help, it also happened that Herat was under siege. The Russians had encouraged the Persian shah to snatch Herat while Dost Muhammad was struggling to secure the Afghan throne. Alarmed by this indirect Russian threat to their northwestern borders, the British sent an officer and some assistance to Herat under orders to stand firm until a diplomatic solution could be worked out. The Afghans in Herat resisted the Persian siege for nine months, while Dost Muhammad worried about the Pushtuns in Peshawar falling under Sikh control. When the British politely refused to stop the Sikhs, the Afghan amir approached the Russian czar for help in retrieving Peshawar. Now thoroughly alarmed, the British governor general decided that protection of British India against Russia required a "friendly government" in Kabul. They turned to the deposed ruler, Shah Shuja, who was willing to let the Sikhs have Peshawar if the British would return him to the Afghan throne.

The First Afghan War

Although the Persians had by then withdrawn from Herat, the British invaded Afghanistan. The First Afghan War (1838–1842) was launched in the southern Helmand Valley. The British forces took Kandahar and Ghazni. Dost Muhammad, finding himself surrounded by plots and

Amir Dost Muhammad.   Nancy Hatch Dupree, *Afghanistan*, Oxford: S. Gupta, 1972.

This extract from Rudyard Kipling's *Many Inventions* is a
tongue-in-check explanation of how the British military tried to
deal with the Afghan tribes. Not understanding Afghan culture,
the British saw the tribesmen playing a naughty and provocative
game. The assumption by the British that they could beat the
Afghans on their own ground helped contribute to the two bloody
Afghan wars.

. . . The Afghans were always a secretive race, and vastly
preferred doing something wicked to saying nothing at all. They
would be quiet and well-behaved for months, till one night, without
word or warning, they would rush a police-post, cut the throats of a
constable or two, dash through a village, carry away three or four
women, and withdraw, in the red glare of burning thatch, driving
the cattle and goats before them to their own desolate hills. The
Indian Government would become almost tearful on these occasions.
First it would say, "Please be good and we'll forgive you." The
tribe concerned in the latest depredation would collectively put its
thumb to its nose and answer rudely. Then the Government would
say: "Hadn't you better pay up a little money for those few corpses
you left behind you the other night?" Here the tribe would
temporise, and lie and bully, and some of the younger men, merely
to show contempt of authority, would raid another police post and
fire into some frontier mud fort, and, if lucky, kill a real English
officer. Then the Government would say: "Observe; if you really

persist in this line of conduct you will be hurt." If the tribe knew exactly what was going on in India, it would apologise or be rude, according as it learned whether the Government was busy with other things, or able to devote its full attention to their performances. Some of the tribes knew to one corpse how far to go. Others became excited, lost their heads, and told the Government to come on. With sorrow and tears, and one eye on the British taxpayer at home, who insisted on regarding these exercises as brutal wars of annexation, the Government would prepare an expensive little field-brigade and some guns, and send all up into the hills to chase the wicked tribe out of the valleys, where the corn grew, into the hill-tops where there was nothing to eat. The tribe would turn out in full strength and enjoy the campaign, for they knew that their women would never be touched, that their wounded would be nursed, not mutilated, and that as soon as each man's bag of corn was spent they could surrender and palaver with the English General as though they had been a real enemy. Afterwards, years afterwards, they would pay the blood-money, driblet by driblet, to the Government and tell their children how they had slain redcoats by thousands. The only drawback to this kind of picnic-war was the weakness of the redcoats for solemnly blowing up with powder their fortified towers and keeps. This the tribe always considered mean.

Excerpt from "The Lost Legion" in *Many Inventions* by Rudyard Kipling (London: Macmillan and Co., Ltd, 1907), pp. 185–186.

intrigue in Kabul, fled into exile.

The British garrisoned Kabul and put Shah Shuja on the throne, but they failed to realize that Afghan allegiance was not to a throne but to a chief among chieftains. In a situation very similar to that of the Russian-supported government in Kabul in the 1980s, the reinstated Shah Shuja was a puppet monarch supported by foreign troops, who soon found themselves the target of bloody resistance. The British garrison, harassed on all sides by rebellious Afghans, decided in January 1842 that it must evacuate. Afghan leaders in Kabul guaranteed that the British troops might go unmolested into India, but the Afghan leaders in Kabul were not the recognized leaders of the Afghan tribes in the rugged mountains along the evacuation route.

The British column—4,500 fighting men, a number of women and children, and 12,500 camp followers—moved out of Kabul in the deep snow and bitter cold of midwinter, down through the rock-strewn defiles and narrow icy passes. They were immediately attacked by vengeful hill tribes and massacred before they could reach the Jalalabad plain.

A British expedition returned within the year to Kabul to avenge the massacre. They burned the citadel and the great bazaar, recovered captives and hostages held by the Afghans, crushed all opposition in the field—and then departed. Their attempt to establish a protectorate in Afghanistan, at a tremendous expense in both money and men, had achieved little more than the lasting enmity and bitterness of the Afghans.

Shah Shuja had been murdered during the campaign by his own followers. After the British withdrew from Afghanistan, they released Dost Muhammad from exile. He returned to Kabul and was welcomed by his countrymen. Before he died in 1863, he succeeded in unifying Afghanistan in about the form it is today.

In the struggle for power among Dost Muhammad's sons, Sher Ali eventually succeeded to the throne in 1868. During his reign negotiations between London and St. Petersburg resulted in a loose agreement that Russia would respect the northern boundary of Afghanistan as roughly on the Oxus River, and that the country to the south was outside the sphere of Russian influence.

Difficulties flared between Britain and Russia in 1877, however, and were disastrous to Sher Ali. The Russians moved troops to the Afghan border and in 1878 dispatched a diplomatic mission to the Afghan amir. Immediately the British dispatched a countermission, but Afghan border guards stopped the group at the Khyber Pass. Greatly incensed, the British demanded that the Afghans apologize and allow their envoy to proceed. The amir's explanation did not satisfy them, and the Second Afghan War began.

Afghan soldiers from the period of the wars with England.   Nancy Hatch Dupree, *Afghanistan,* Oxford: S. Gupta, 1972.

The Second Afghan War

Sher Ali appealed for Russian aid when the British invaded his country from the south, but none was forthcoming. Leaving affairs in Kabul in the hands of his son Yakub Khan, Sher Ali fled north to seek help, only to be advised by the Russians to return to his capital and make peace with the British. He died in Mazar-i-Sharif a few months later, a broken man.

The British forces quickly defeated the Afghans, but they repeated the mistake they had made in the First Afghan War—relying on the wrong leader. Yakub Khan may have been the amir's son, and he was in charge of government affairs in Kabul, but he was not the accepted chief of all the chiefs. He acceded to all the British demands, the main one being that Afghanistan must conduct relations with foreign states in accordance with the advice of the British government. The British representatives sent to Kabul in 1879 as the result of the peace treaty were murdered by rebellious Afghans a few weeks later. The three British armies still intact moved forward immediately and occupied Kabul and Kandahar. Shortly thereafter Yakub Khan went into exile.

This was the furthest extent of British "forward policy," based on the concept that protection of British India against Russia required the British to control the natural frontiers all the way to the northern slopes of the Hindu Kush. It had, however, now become very apparent that British occupation of those rugged mountains was not practical, both because of the tremendous expense involved in maintaining troops so far from Indian bases, and because of the hostility of the people of this remote area to outside authority. A dozen different tribes were by now mounting full-scale war against the British.

The alternative seemed to be for the British to find among the Afghan chiefs a leader who would be acceptable both to the British and to the

Afghans. Amazingly enough, this slender hope was rewarded by the appearance on the Oxus of Sirdar Abdur Rahman, nephew of the exiled amir and grandson of Dost Muhammad. The tribes of Afghan Turkistan rallied to his side. The British immediately relinquished the control they had won in the Second Afghan War and withdrew. Abdur Rahman paid for British recognition by surrendering control of Afghanistan's foreign affairs to the British.

Amir Abdur Rahman

Abdur Rahman had been almost twelve years in Russian exile, and wore a Russian uniform when he rode into Kabul. The British gambled that he would resist any Russian interference in his affairs just as fiercely as his predecessors had resisted the British. The success of this gamble, which made Afghanistan a buffer state between Russia and British India, was in no small measure due to the wisdom of the amir himself, for he understood very well the role he was to play.

During his reign the British and Russians reached a settlement of the whole long border between Russia and Afghanistan from the Pamirs to Iran. The border between Afghanistan and British India to the southeast was also demarcated by the famous Durand Line, which clarified the respective areas in which the Afghans and the British would be responsible for controlling the Pushtun tribes living on the frontier. Unfortunately, the Durand Line cut the lands of the Pushtun tribes in half. The resulting conflict of interest has led to an endless series of border raids, punitive expeditions, and constant intriguing back and forth across the border—perpetuated in the 1980s by guerrilla bands fighting the Soviet occupation and communist government in Kabul.

Abdur Rahman's achievements during his reign were impressive. His main task was the integration of rebellious tribes into a single polity.

He weakened the autonomy of the tribes by transferring many of the military and administrative functions of the chiefs to the central government. He transferred loyal tribesmen as settlers into rebellious regions, and crushed the Hazarahs and Nuristanis by invading their lands. The amir imposed his authority with an iron hand, but a less drastic rule could not have merged his diverse peoples under centralized rule.

In 1901 Abdur Rahman's eldest son, Habibullah, his chosen and trained heir, succeeded his father. Habibullah continued his father's isolationist policy and consistently rejected all attempts by foreign interests to gain concessions in Afghanistan. During the years that Habibullah ruled Afghanistan, however, he introduced western medicine, abolished slavery, and founded a college on European lines.

In the 1907 Convention of St. Petersburg, Britain and Russia reiterated their agreement that Afghanistan should remain a buffer state. When World War I broke out, Afghanistan felt considerable pressure from both sides. The Germans intrigued for Afghan help against Britain; the sultan of Turkey (who considered himself head of the Moslem faith) called for *jihad* (holy war) against the allies; and leaders of the Indian independence movement attempted to involve Afghanistan in the hostilities. Although he incurred strong animosity among his people for doing so, the amir loyally abided by his agreement with Great Britain to maintain strict neutrality. In return he requested complete independence for his country when the war ended. After the war, before any public agreement came from the British, internal political intrigue culminated in Habibullah's assassination in 1919.

His third son, Amanullah, held the capital, the treasury, and the arsenal at the time of his father's death. He seized control and was accepted as amir without any serious disturbances.

Feeling in Afghanistan ran high, however, because of the widespread conviction that the British owed the Afghans independence in return for their neutrality in World War I. To bolster his shaky regime, Amanullah launched the Third Afghan War against the British in 1919, capitalizing on the rising anticolonial sentiments among his people. Troop movements against India were begun in the Khyber, Khost, and Kandahar areas. Immediate reverses in the Khyber and airplane bombings by the British of Jalalabad and Kabul made a profound impression in the capital. Within ten days a truce was requested. The British Government, exhausted by the World War, accepted with some relief. It was now clear that the Afghans would not remain subordinate unless Britain forced them to. To the north the Bolsheviks (communists) were too preoccupied with their struggle to gain control of Russia after the overthrow of the czar to meddle in Afghanistan.

Independence

Therefore, in the peace treaty of Rawalpindi signed in 1921, the British granted a major policy victory to the Afghans by returning control of Afghanistan's foreign affairs to the Afghan monarch.

Having gained the independence he wanted so badly, Amanullah quickly abandoned his father's distrust of foreign ideas and introduced a series of drastic reforms patterned on European models in an effort to modernize his country. The reforms themselves do not appear very radical today, but Amanullah's method of undertaking them led to his downfall. His country's revenue was negligible; his army neglected and underpaid. There was only a handful of educated, literate Afghans who understood what he wanted to do. His new administrative code conflicted with the established canons of Islamic law, and his plans for the rapid emancipation and education of women infuriated the people and the Moslem religious leaders.

Matters came to a sudden head in 1928 when a minor tribal incident developed into a full-scale rebellion among the eastern and southern tribes. This conflict provided the opportunity for a brigand from the north named Bacha-i-Saquo—Son of the Water Carrier—to gather a band of followers and advance on Kabul. Amanullah, deserted by his poorly paid soldiers, abdicated and fled to India in 1929.

Bacha seized Kabul and began a period of appalling terror, torture, and extortion. Afghanistan was rescued from this new curse by a great-grandson of a brother of Dost Muhammad.

Nadir Shah

Nadir Khan had served in Amir Habibullah's royal bodyguard, and eventually rose to be commander-in-chief of the army. When Habibullah was assassinated, Nadir Khan continued to serve Aminullah for some years, but he was living in virtual exile in France when the news of Kabul's capture by Bacha-i-Saquo reached him. Nadir Khan immediately sailed for India. Without funds, and at first without either foreign or tribal support, he and his brothers journeyed to the Khost frontier to rally the tribes. There ensued a period of urgent negotiation, of tribal jealousies, treachery, and the reviving of ancient feuds, of wavering and uncertainty as to whether to follow Nadir Khan. He finally won enough support among tribesmen on the Indian side of the frontier to defeat Bacha and seize Kabul. An assembly of tribal chiefs proclaimed him "King of all the Afghans."

The situation was a precarious one: The treasury was empty. Several thousand triumphant tribesmen were hungry for loot. The most immediate task was to restore order and establish central authority. Nadir Shah set up a new administration based on orthodox Islamic law and outlined plans to develop his country. During his brief reign internal revenue was raised, a 40,000-man army created, a road built through the Hindu

Kush, and the highways of the country made safer than they had ever been before.

In spite of the king's vigilant efforts to root out opposition, the son of a servant of an executed conspirator shot King Nadir Shah at a school-prize competition in 1933. For once family solidarity overrode personal ambition in Afghanistan, and the dead king's brothers took immediate steps to ensure the accession of his son to the throne.

Zahir Shah

Zahir Shah was nineteen at the time of his accession—still very young to assume control of so turbulent a country. In keeping with Afghan tradition, the late king's brothers assumed control, although they did not contest the throne. The power struggles of the past were abandoned.

The 1931 constitution of Zahir Shah's father continued as the legal foundation of Afghan government for the next thirty years. On paper that constitution provided for a constitutional monarchy, but the document was a somewhat contradictory mélange of Moslem law, local tradition, and democratic institutions of Western origin—the whole arranged to maintain the power of the royal family. The various branches of government had no clearly defined, differentiated powers, nor were Afghan citizens protected from arbitrary power of the executive and judiciary. In actuality, the royal government in the years 1933–1963 was an enlightened oligarchy.

In 1953 the king's uncles stepped down, to be replaced by first cousins of the king's generation. Prime Minister Muhammad Daud, himself a professional soldier, and Foreign Minister Naim controlled the administration, the police, and the armed forces for a decade. Other important positions were almost invariably held by members of the royal family, which maintained a pervasive control of national affairs.

In the early 1960s quarrels with Pakistan over the rights of the Pushtun tribes living in the frontier areas led to border closings and severe dislocations in Afghanistan's normal trade. As the border crisis dragged on from 1961 to 1963, it became clear that a change in cabinet policy was necessary to negotiate the reopening of the trade routes to the Indian subcontinent. At the king's request Prime Minister Daud quietly stepped down from his powerful position at the head of the government. (The policies of the 1960s are discussed in more detail in the next chapter.)

In appointing the new prime minister and council of ministers, the king excluded all members of the Afghan royal family for the first time. At the same time, he announced that a new constitution would replace that of 1931. Clearly he had decided that the time had come to bring the educated people of the country into the governing process.

The constitution that was written and approved in 1964 by a *Loya Jirgah* (a national convening of the tribal chiefs and other leaders) was a far more precise document than its predecessor, creating separate and independent executive, legislative, and judicial branches, excluding all close relatives of the king from high office, and providing for the establishment of political parties and a free press. Unfortunately, its implementation was left in the hands of the small group of educated people at the top, with the result that the Afghan people developed little sense of loyalty to the new political system.

The new parliament *(Wolesi Jirgah)* suffered particularly from its members' lack of understanding of their legislative function. The deputies were largely conservative landowners or tribal and religious leaders from rural areas, who had little experience with constitutional government. The body devoted far more time and attention to investigating and demanding explanations from the executive branch than to passing the bills put before it.

At the same time prime ministers and their councils of ministers found it very difficult to exercise any dynamic leadership under the new constitution. They were frequently harassed by parliament, which was supposed to approve their appointment by the king. Political parties were never legally formed, because the king feared that politics might get out of control if he signed the laws that permitted the formation of political parties. The lack of any organized support in the legislature for their programs prevented government officials from implementing effective policies.

Power remained, consequently, very much in the hands of the king, who not only frequently exerted personal pressure on deputies to get bills through parliament, but also governed by royal decree when parliament failed to pass budgets and other bills. In spite of laws guaranteeing a free press, several of the opposition newspapers that dared to criticize the government were shut down as being contrary to the public interest. Latent dissatisfaction with national affairs found expression from time to time in strikes and demonstrations, particularly among the university students and faculty.

The Afghan army and air force, very well organized and efficiently trained with U.S.S.R. assistance, were the power behind the throne. The king's cousin, the same Muhammad Daud who had served as prime minister from 1953 to 1963, maintained close contact and strong influence with the military officers. He watched the bungling and inefficiency in parliament and the government bureaucracy until it became intolerable. When a severe drought in 1971–1972 worsened economic conditions as well, he took advantage of the absence of Zahir Shah on a trip to Europe to seize control of the government in a relatively bloodless military coup.

The immediate favorable reactions of military officers and much of the educated elite (including a small core of clandestine communists) were a good indication of their dissatisfaction with the failure of the king to provide the support his ministers needed to make constitutional democracy work and their optimism that Daud would be a strong leader. He proclaimed the end of the monarchy and the creation of a republic, with himself as first president and prime minister.

Revolution

No one made decisions that had more influence on the destiny of modern Afghanistan than Muhammad Daud. His decision to champion the cause of the Pushtuns beyond the Durand Line when the British withdrew from India in 1947 led to quarrels with neighboring Pakistan and negated the possibility of American military aid. His decision to seek Soviet help in the 1950s for modernizing the Afghan military moved his country into the Russian sphere of influence. His decision to end the monarchy in 1973 reintroduced the idea that dissatisfied factions could intrigue outside of the legal process to gain control of the country. His appointment of left-wing radicals who advocated Marxist-Leninist programs to his first cabinet gave the small group of Afghan communists a status that the law had denied them. And his decision in

Young boys in Logar play at being resistance fighters.   Ed Grazda

the mid-1970s to reduce his country's dependence on the U.S.S.R.
alarmed the Kremlin. In the end, those decisions cost Daud his life and
his country its independence.

The Pushtunistan Issue

Daud and other royal leaders in Kabul saw the creation of Pakistan in
1947 as an opportunity to champion the cause of their ethnic brothers,
the Pushtuns whose territory had been part of British India. They
claimed that the Durand Line had been forced on Amir Abdur Rahman
by the British and was not a valid international frontier. They held that

the Pushtun people of the two Pakistan provinces along Afghanistan's border (the North-West Frontier Province and Baluchistan) should be given the choice not only of joining either independent India or Pakistan, but also of joining Afghanistan or becoming independent. In the 1947 referendum, the Pushtun tribesmen either abstained (some of them because the choice was limited to Pakistan or India and did not include self-determination) or indicated overwhelming preference for Pakistan, which was to be a Moslem state. The British therefore transferred sovereignty over the frontier provinces and their largely Pushtun population to the new Pakistan government.

The Pakistan government saw no reason to offer independence to the Pushtuns in the frontier provinces if the Pushtuns on the Afghan side of the border did not have the same option. Pakistan quickly consolidated and confirmed its authority over the frontier area by calling *jirgahs* of all the most important tribes and making agreements with the individual chiefs. In 1955, after Muhammad Daud became prime minister of Afghanistan, Pakistan undertook a merger of all the provinces of West Pakistan into one administrative unit. The verbal sparring between the two countries then turned into something more serious, for the Afghans interpreted this move as an attempt to end any possibility of an independent Pushtunistan for the Pakistani Pushtuns. Afghan diplomats were recalled from Pakistan, the Afghan army mobilized, and mobs in both countries attacked diplomatic establishments. Pakistan quickly retaliated by applying an unofficial embargo on Afghan transit trade through Pakistan—the normal route to the outside world. Trade was vital to Afghanistan's survival, and the result was a diversion of Afghan trade north through the U.S.S.R.

Tribal raiding across the border led to another border closing in 1961 and halted Afghan trade through Pakistan for two years. It was to end this crisis that King Zahir asked his cousin to relinquish the prime ministership.

During this period Afghanistan's relations with the Soviet Union altered drastically. Before 1951 there was little trade between the two countries. In spite of their long common border, no adequate river ports existed on the Amu Darya. A new relationship was established in 1951, when a four-year commercial treaty was signed. Soviet petroleum products, cotton cloth, sugar, and other important commodities were exchanged for Afghan wool, hides, and cotton. The Soviets permitted free transit of Afghan goods and offered a much higher exchange rate than any Western country could afford.

Soviet Economic and Military Assistance

In 1953 the Soviets offered Afghanistan several small grants for street paving in Kabul, and for building grain storage facilities, a bakery, and oil storage tanks. The Czechs provided assistance for cement plants, a glass factory, a coal-briquetting plant, and a fruit-processing plant.

Nevertheless, before 1955 eighty percent of Afghanistan's exports and imports still passed through Pakistan. When the 1955 quarrel with Pakistan over the status of the Pushtun tribes living along the border halted that trade, the U.S.S.R. rapidly expanded free transit and the supply of goods. By the time mediation by Saudi Arabia led to the lifting of the Pakistani embargo, a large portion of Afghanistan's trade had been shifted north.

At this time Prime Minister Daud, a professional military man himself, was eager to modernize his army and air force. His requests to the United States for military aid were refused because of Washington's military alliance with Pakistan—with whom the Afghan government was quarreling over an independent Pushtunistan.

In 1955 the Soviet leaders, Bulganin and Khrushchev, visited Kabul.

Clearly they viewed the cultivation of a friendly government in Kabul as an important policy in countering the influence of the West in Iran and Pakistan. They announced support of Afghanistan's demand for self-determination for the Pushtuns of Pakistan, then made available to the Afghan leaders a $100 million credit for economic development, to be repaid in barter goods at a nominal 2-percent interest rate over a

A farmer in Bamiyan Province, rifle slung over his shoulder, scatters seed across a rocky field.   Ed Grazda

thirty-year period. The Afghans also requested and received from the Soviet bloc the necessary military assistance to modernize and efficiently train their army and air force.

In the succeeding years the Soviet Union provided not only substantial assistance for economic development projects, but also constructed a major road network, a tunnel through the Hindu Kush to permit year-round transport to the north, a river port and railroad bridge across the Amu Darya, and the airfields needed to operate an efficient air force. Some of these activities were more strategic than economic, aimed at moving Afghanistan permanently into the Russian sphere of influence.

The king and his advisers were fully cognizant of the fact that Afghanistan's armed forces were completely dependent on Russia for matériel and fuel, but in accepting massive Soviet assistance, they gambled on their belief that Afghanistan could walk a middle road between the two superpowers, accepting help from each but maintaining their country's independence by balancing each side against the other. Their confidence was, of course, predicated on the assumption that the Pushtun leaders who had controlled the country since 1747 would continue their rule.

The equation changed when Muhammad Daud ended the monarchy and took personal charge of the government. Abolishing the monarchy may have been Daud's fatal mistake. As a member of the royal family, he could have easily assumed the royal title. The Afghans were accustomed to having a king, and the monarchy was one of the few unifying forces in a very diverse, loosely organized country.

By failing to continue the traditional authority, Daud undermined his own legitimacy and made it easier for commoners to conspire to replace him. His attempts to carry out badly needed economic and social reforms met with little success, and a new constitution promulgated in 1977 permitted only one party to operate legally. Frustrated opponents were further alienated when Daud turned away from the radicals whom he had included in his first government and surrounded himself with traditionalists. Aware that his country was dependent on the U.S.S.R., Daud also began to turn more and more to Iran and Saudi Arabia for economic support.

These moves alarmed the small group of left-wing radicals who had cooperated with Daud in 1973. Although political parties had never been legalized, Zahir Shah's experiment in democracy back in 1964 had encouraged unofficial extremist groups on both the left and right to gather in secret. A communist party, the People's Democratic Party of Afghanistan (P.D.P.A.)—a small group of a few dozen university lecturers, civil servants, and teachers—had been formed in 1965 to contest in the parliamentary elections. It won two seats in the 1969 parliament; one went to Babrak Karmal and the other to Hafizullah Amin—both of whom would later head a communist government in Kabul.

As early as 1967, however, the party split into two factions, followed by a decade of antagonistic competition for the loyalties of the small group of radical leftists in the country. Some of their differences were based on differing philosophies. The Khalq (people's party) faction was largely from modest provincial families, mainly Pushtun, with a working-class orientation, strongly nationalistic, bent on forming a Leninist working-class party. Members of the Parcham (flag party) faction were generally urban dwellers, speakers of Farsi, better educated and more emancipated, trying to form a broad nationalist front that could work within the system.

The Saur Revolution

Although Daud had used left-wing military officers to spearhead his 1973 coup, had welcomed left-wing support for his new republic, and had brought P.D.P.A. leaders into the government (including appointments to half his first cabinet posts), he soon became disenchanted with their demands and with student unrest and strikes and demonstrations led by left-wing radicals. After 1975 Daud dismissed his Parcham ministers and began seeking economic assistance from the Shah of Iran. In 1977 he formed a new cabinet of extreme conservatives, which may

A mujahid *commander climbs a rocky trail. The forested mountains in the background are found only in northeastern Afghanistan.* Christopher Brown

have played a role in causing Khalq and Parcham to end their ten-year schism in 1978. It became clear that their opposition to Daud's conservative turn was behind much of the agitation on the Kabul University campus.

A series of political assassinations in Kabul in 1977 and 1978 finally alarmed Daud to the point that he ordered the arrest of the communist leaders, confident that the military would not be influenced by the clandestine base of support that Hafizullah Amin had been building among some of the army and air force officers. Warned by Amin and expecting Daud to move against them, these officers initiated a bloody coup that assassinated Daud and most of the ruling family. Because the coup took place in April (Saur in the local language), it has been tagged the Saur Revolution.

Into the vacuum stepped the newly united P.D.P.A.—a few hundred men with only a tiny following, little popular support, and an aspiration to create a modern society by means of social revolution. Curiously enough, of the members of the first postrevolution cabinet, ten had attended schools in the United States, while only four (three of them military officers) had been trained in the Soviet Union. Yet the P.D.P.A. looked to the U.S.S.R. as its model and friend.

The P.D.P.A. leaders established the Democratic Republic of Afghanistan, with Nur Muhammad Taraki (an Afghan Pushtun writer who had learned Marxism at night school while working in India), secretary general of the P.D.P.A., as president of the Revolutionary Council and prime minister. At first, this new government seemed a welcome relief after the disappointments of the Daud regime, for it promised agrarian reforms and a more democratic society. Peasant debts were canceled by decree and ethnic minorities promised respect.

The coalition government held together barely three months, however, before the Khalqis started replacing the Parchami leaders. Babrak Karmal was sent to Prague as ambassador; others were purged or

imprisoned. Civil servants were ordered to join the P.D.P.A. if they wanted to keep their jobs. Party members were substituted for all suspect government officials. The history of Afghanistan was rewritten to condemn the dynasty of Nadir Shah for all the ills of the country and trace the legitimacy of the new government's reform plans back to King Amanullah. Older military officers were retired and mass promotions granted to younger party loyalists. A program of giving land to the rural farmers was instituted, ignoring all the traditional rules that governed credit and water rights.

Within the year Taraki signed a Treaty of Friendship, Good Neighborliness, and Cooperation with Moscow. The entire Afghan economy was placed under central control and a bold Five Year Plan announced, with $1 billion in Soviet aid promised to finance it. Taraki moved his country into the Soviet orbit, confident that the military could keep him in power. In the previous two decades some 10,000 junior military officers (from an army of 80,000 and an air force of 10,000) had gone to the Soviet Union or its satellites for training. These officers were not converted to communism, but many of them returned with heightened awareness of social injustice and strong feelings against the traditional establishment.

The new leaders had no strong links with tribes or ethnic groups in any part of the country, and they proved grossly insensitive in dealing with rural communities. Opposition to the Marxist government developed almost immediately. Most Afghans opposed the new government's left-wing "reform" program, which ignored their deeply rooted traditions and their strong religious orientation. A major revolt in Nuristan province a few months later was the first step in an insurgency that

A group of resistance fighters in Paktia Province with a captured Soviet antiaircraft gun.
Christopher Brown

gradually spread across the entire country. Mass oppression was instituted to control it. Differences between the P.D.P.A.'s two factions increased, and in October the Parchami leaders who had been sent abroad as ambassadors (including Babrak Karmal and Muhammad Najibullah) were dismissed and found havens in Eastern Europe.

Hafizullah Amin, a teacher with a master's degree from Teachers College of Columbia University, took over Taraki's duties as prime minister early in 1979, but by fall a dispute between the two resulted in Amin having Taraki killed and assuming complete power. In spite of Amin's muting some of the brashly socialist elements of his policies, as well as promoting a return to Islam in an attempt to assuage his countrymen's strong spiritual sensibilities, his new strategy of reconciliation convinced few Afghan refugees to return from Iran or Pakistan. The resort to mass imprisonment and killing of opponents continued. The publication in November of 12,000 names of prisoners who had died in the year since the revolution in a single Kabul prison led for the first time to guerrilla attacks within the city of Kabul.

The mounting instability at the top fueled the growing insurgency in the countryside. Tribal chiefs abandoned their loyalty to the central government. Fundamentalist Moslem leaders, fired by the recent success of a religious revolution in Iran, reacted against the atheistic policies of the Khalqi leaders. The urban population was outraged by mass imprisonments and indiscriminate executions. Most serious of all, the Afghan army—the only glue that held the country together now—began to disintegrate in protest against orders to put down the rebellion among its own countrymen. Many soldiers deserted and took their arms with them to join the resistance. The Kabul government no longer controlled the rural hinterland away from the towns and highways. The desperate Amin had only fresh shipments of advanced Soviet arms and his thousands of Soviet advisers to fall back on.

Mujahidin *pause to rest near a typical Afghan village.*   Ed Grazda

The Soviet Invasion

The fact that the country was on the brink of disintegration was not lost on the Soviet advisers. Russia had aspired for two centuries to control this important borderland and had invested two decades of its prestige in furthering that goal. Clearly, if the U.S.S.R. did not act now, those twenty years of investment in and cultivation of this southern neighbor would have been wasted. On the night of December 24, 1979, large numbers of Soviet airborne forces landed and took over the Kabul airport and key points in the city. Columns of tanks and troops crossed the northern border—the first time since World War II that Russian soldiers had entered a country that did not belong to the Warsaw Pact.

On December 27 Hafizullah Amin was assassinated. In his place the Soviets installed Babrak Karmal, the son of an army officer, who had become a left-wing militant while a student at Kabul University. He was the leader of the Parcham faction of the P.D.P.A., had been in exile, and was flown in from the Soviet Union. The official Soviet position was that they were responding to a call for assistance from the Afghan government under the 1978 Treaty of Friendship, Good Neighborliness, and Cooperation between the two countries.

Within weeks the massive Soviet military operation brought in 85,000 troops—equivalent to the entire Afghan army. But even with this new support, and an untold number of Soviet advisers and technicians, Babrak Karmal had little more success than his predecessors in establishing his authority much beyond the capital city. Two thirds of the Afghan army disappeared into the countryside as demonstrations and strikes paralyzed the cities. Thousands of resisters were executed, and western journalists were evicted from the country. Guerrilla fighting continued in almost all the twenty-nine provinces. The cities of Herat and Kandahar were bombed repeatedly in a vain attempt to regain control from the resistance, and regular sorties mounted against the *mujahidin* in the rural countryside. The Afghans refused to accept socialist principles or to mute their anger at being controlled by a foreign army.

As the guerrilla war stretched from months into years, indications of Soviet displeasure with Karmal's regime mounted, including relatively direct criticism in the Soviet press. In May of 1986, after returning from "medical treatment" in the Soviet Union, Karmal announced that he was stepping down as P.D.P.A. general secretary and being replaced by Lieutenant General Muhammad Najibullah, former chief of the Afghan secret police (KHAD) and a Parcham who had been in exile in Eastern Europe with Karmal.

Later in 1986 Najibullah also assumed the post of ceremonial president of the Revolutionary Council, concentrating total power in his hands. He had established a reputation for grim, brutal efficiency during his tenure as KHAD chief. A Pushtun himself, he devoted considerable effort to sowing dissension among the Pushtun tribes that provided a substantial portion of the *mujahidin* fighters. The Soviets obviously expected him to take a firmer hold than his predecessors in party, government, and military affairs.

The acting chief of state, Hajji Muhammad Chamkani, was chosen to give religious sanction to the new regime. The title *hajji* indicates that he has made the Moslem pilgrimage to Mecca and is a respected religious figure. In its effort to win support, Najibullah's government cultivated Moslem religious leaders and claimed to have more than 10,000 of them on its payroll.

None of these steps won the support that the communist government in Kabul needed. In the face of determined resistance and heavy losses, the Soviets announced in February 1988 that they would withdraw their army and leave the Afghans to work out their own political problems.

Honor and Faith

The period in which the ideas of the modern world have been welcomed in Afghanistan barely exceeds half a century. The transistor radio in the village teahouse and the gaudily decorated trucks on the main highways bring awareness that another way of life exists, but they do not change the deeply ingrained outlook of the rural farmers and herdsmen. Only a small stratum of urban dwellers, who have benefitted from education and participation in the newly developed economic sector, is eager to move Afghanistan out of its traditional ways and transform it into a more modern society.

The clash between the two outlooks has caused difficulties for the Afghan leadership ever since King Amanullah assumed the throne in 1919. Even today, much of the conflict between the revolutionary leaders of the Republic of Afghanistan and the resistance groups is a conflict between the push for rapid modernization and the traditional social patterns that regulate much of Afghan life. The radical leaders and their Soviet advisers have regarded the tribesmen as primitive bandits who must be forced to adopt more progressive ways, while the tribal leaders and Moslem theologians have believed that the government was intent on destroying both their spiritual values and their independence. The civil war resulted from this conflict in outlook, and its emotional focus was sharpened by the interference of foreign troops in a family quarrel.

An understanding of the very narrow outlook of the bulk of the Afghans, most of them extremely poor, requires an awareness of the rules that govern their lives. Despite the country's ethnic diversity, 99 percent of the Afghans are Moslems, and most of them have been shaped by shared ancient tribal traditions, either those of their own ethnic group or of the dominant Pushtuns. Islam itself developed in a similar tribal society in Arabia, where the rules were dictated by a harsh desert climate and very limited resources, and the Moslem concepts of equality, courage, and honor matched the code that governed life in the Hindu Kush before the Arabs arrived.

Tribal Code

The tribe in Afghanistan is a related group of extended families and clans who can all trace their genealogy to common ancestors, whose name the tribe shares. The Afridis and Mohmands and Warrakzais mentioned in the poetry of Khushal Khan Khattak in an earlier chapter are examples of Pushtun tribes. The tribal organization may be further divided into subtribes *(kheyl)*, each headed by its own chief. The families and clans generally live in adjacent villages or travel and herd their flocks together if they are nomads.

Tribal law in this part of the world is as old as society itself. It is more than a set of rules. It is a way of life, evolved over the centuries by pastoral peoples living in desert climates all the way from the Mediterranean to far Mongolia. It recognizes the need for an established authority to maintain the unity of the tribe, and it defines the rules of behavior in the tribesmen's relations with each other.

Since the Pushtuns are the largest ethnic group and have provided the rulers of modern Afghanistan, their tribal code, *Pushtunwali*, dominates the national outlook. It is of unknown origin and age, and has been handed down by word of mouth from generation to generation as a basic part of family training. Every Pushtun child is so carefully taught the principles of this code that it becomes an integral part of his or her character at an early age. The penalty for disobeying the code may be ostracism, expulsion from the tribe, or even death, and very few risk such consequences.

Pushtunwali covers a wide area of human behavior. The most important principles deal with honor, revenge, and hospitality.

The personal honor *(ghayrat)* of the Puhstun is regarded as more important than life itself, and the coward or traitor is the most despised of men. This matter of honor starts with the individual, and requires the tribesman to keep his promise at any cost and regardless of the circumstances under which it was given. It extends to the family, where every member feels compelled to uphold family prestige, and dishonoring the family name is the blackest of crimes. In its broadest sense, honor extends to the whole tribe and is the responsibility of every member of the tribe.

This concept of tribal honor has been responsible for the Pushtuns' reputation as fighters and raiders. The raid, which in other parts of the world is considered a form of brigandage, became a respected tribal institution in nomadic society. The crucial importance of water and pasturage made the tribes competitors for these limited resources. In the struggle for survival, raiding became one of the most manly of occupations, and an extensive set of rules grew up to cover the planning of raids and their successful and heroic execution. Bravery is regarded as an indispensable quality for every Pushtun, and every tribesman must return from battle victorious or die on the field in the attempt.

Related to the principle of honor is that of revenge *(badal)*. Badal requires a tribesman to seek redress for a wrong done to him by taking revenge on his wrongdoer. Every crime—be it cattle rustling, wife stealing, adultery, or whatever—has a whole set of complex rules measuring the proper revenge. The tribesman is duty bound to pursue his revenge until he has secured adequate justice against the man who has harmed him or sullied his honor. In fact, revenge may become the obligation of a whole family, clan, or tribe, and it may be executed against any members of the guilty man's family, even carrying over from generation to generation. The blood feuds that have resulted from this kind of vengeance are the source of many dramatic tales in Pushtun oral history.

On the other side of the coin is the principle of hospitality *(milmastia)*. The tribesmen's awareness of the dangers of life in barren mountains and burning desert turns hospitality into a sacred duty. The guest may be a stranger to the land, or a neighboring tribesman, or even a bitter enemy, but if he needs shelter and sustenance and has come as a guest, it is the duty of every tribesman to welcome and protect him. In return, every tribesman can expect the same welcome and protection when he is away from his own people.

The traveler in Afghanistan never lacks for food and shelter if he seeks it in the spirit in which it is so generously given. The Afghans' usual reaction to the foreigner is one of friendly curiosity and dignified hospitality, but by no means an uncritical acceptance. Their battle-scarred past and militant tribal traditions rouse strong feelings about any foreign intrusion into what they consider their own affairs.

Pushtunwali also emphasizes the equality of every tribesman and his inherent self-respect. The code places great stress on individual liberty and on freedom of thought and action. On the other hand, having exercised his freedom of choice in assembly with his fellows *(jirgah)*, the tribesman is then required to follow and obey his chosen leaders.

Loyalty is deeply ingrained in the Afghan character. National pride flows from traditional beliefs, from the Moslem faith that almost all Afghans follow, and from the sense that the Afghan nation should stand stalwart and unyielding against any foreign foe. Only when their rulers are identified with strong tribal concepts of tradition and honor will the Afghans give their loyal support to the government in Kabul. The imposition of rulers not of the tribesmen's choosing contributed to the incredible resistance mustered against the P.D.P.A. government and the Soviet invasion.

This kind of patriotism is different from ours. In considering the national attitudes of the Afghans, we must remember that the vast majority of the people are both illiterate and poverty-stricken. Their lives are focused on the hard business of finding food and shelter for their families. Their world is a small one, seldom extending much beyond the confines of the isolated village, the narrow valley, or the tribal grazing ground. What contact they do have with the outside world is through traders and travelers who pass their way, or from the news that reaches them by radio from Kabul, Pakistan, Moscow, or London. Thus their idea of the Afghan nation is less identified with the geographic area that is Afghanistan than with their rulers. Obeying rulers they have not chosen and do not respect offends their deepest sense of honor.

Religious Beliefs

Islam, the religion of the Prophet Muhammad, is professed by almost all of the Afghan population. The masses of the people find that their religion fits their lives and needs. It is no coincidence that Islam and tribal law agree on most basic issues of Afghan life. This religion and this way of life came centuries ago from the same background, the same need of establishing a set of rules that would help a pastoral people to survive in a barren countryside. The fact that the divinely revealed scriptures of the Koran echoed so much of tribal code only made Islam more attractive. Thus, the rural Afghans accept the religion to which they were born and life as it comes and cling to their long-established customs. Resistance to change will continue for the foreseeable future.

In common with tribal law, the Moslem religion stresses the equality and freedom of the individual, at the same time providing a rule of law to govern his actions. The democratic spirit of Islam is quickly felt in Afghanistan. The Afghan stands proudly erect, and servility toward other men is noticeably absent.

The word *Islam* means literally submission to the one true God (Allah—from the Arabic *al-ilah,* meaning "the Supreme Being") and His will. The first pillar of Islam is the profession of this faith: "There is no God but Allah, and Muhammad is His Prophet." Afghan Moslems proclaim this belief daily and follow the teachings of the Koran, the holy book of Islam.

This book is believed by Moslems everywhere to have been revealed to Muhammad (who lived in Arabia from 571 to 632) by the Angel Gabriel. Muhammad is regarded as the last and greatest of the prophets, the line of which began with Adam and continued through Noah, Abraham, Moses, David, Solomon, Jesus, and Muhammad.

The profession of faith already mentioned is an integral part of the second pillar of Islam, prayer. Five times a day—at dawn, at noon, at midafternoon, at sunset, and at the end of the day—the call to prayer comes from the nearest mosque minaret. All devout Afghans cease whatever they are doing, wherever they may be, and kneel facing toward the Arabian city of Mecca to pray. Women pray in the privacy of their homes, but men pray openly in public. This ritual of prayer is performed with a complete lack of self-consciousness, be it in congregation in a mosque courtyard, on a prayer rug in a garden, on a newspaper by a busy city street, or in a circle of stones by a mountain trail. Even the buses and trucks in Afghanistan halt along the road at the correct time while the passengers follow the prayer ritual of a leader chosen among their number.

The third pillar is almsgiving, or charity. In Afghanistan this is

---

Extract from the Koran, Chapter 4, on the proper way to live:

4:35   Serve Allah and associate none with Him. Show kindness to your parents and your kindred, to the orphans and to the needy, to your near and distant neighbors, to your fellow-travellers, to the wayfarers, and to the slaves whom you own. Allah does not love arrogant and boastful men, who are themselves niggardly and enjoin others to be niggardly also; who conceal the riches which Allah of His bounty has bestowed upon them (we have prepared a shameful punishment for the unbelievers); and who spend their wealth for the sake of ostentation, believing neither in Allah nor in the Last Day. He that chooses Satan for his friend, an evil friend has he.

Translation from Arabic to English by N. J. Dawood (New York: Penguin Books, 1956)

practiced through the closely integrated kinship system, wherein families take care of their own. In addition, every man pays a village tax for the poor and another to support the *mullah*, the religious leader in charge of the mosque.

The fourth pillar is fasting. During the lunar month of Ramazan (Ramadan) no food or liquid is eaten between dawn and sunset. This is an act of considerable devotion in itself, but when Ramazan occurs in midsummer, the torrid heat of the Afghan deserts makes the denial of even a drop of water an extreme sacrifice. Ramazan, the ninth month of the Moslem lunar calendar, is honored thus because it is the month in which the Koran was revealed to Muhammad.

The fifth pillar is the pilgrimage *(hajj)* to Mecca, which every Moslem tries to make at least once in his lifetime as the final stamp of his faith. Mecca was both the city of Muhammad's birth and a famous pilgrimage spot long before his birth. In his doctrine Muhammad traced the Meccan sanctuary that is the center of the faith back to the biblical Abraham and dedicated it to the one Supreme Being. The pilgrimage to Mecca serves as a common bond among Moslems all over the world. Afghan pilgrims make the *hajj* on special buses or on chartered flights of Ariana Afghan Airlines.

Muhammad was considerably influenced by both Judaism and Christianity, both of which had in his lifetime a substantial following in the Arabian Peninsula. He called the Christians and the Jews "People of the Book," meaning that they too believed in divine scriptures. And like them, he taught his people that there was only one supreme God, to whose will men should submit. Moslem belief in the basic goodness of man as a creature of God gives the devout Afghan a feeling of confidence and contentment. The reward is a peaceful soul and the promise of happiness in paradise after death.

Four fifths of Afghan Moslems are of the orthodox Sunni sect, while one fifth are Shiah, a sect that broke away from the mainstream of Islam as the result of disputes over who should succeed Muhammad as the leader (caliph) of the faithful, rather than from any conflict over beliefs.

Afghan boys attend a village school.   United Nations

The Shiah repudiated the first three caliphs and sponsored Muhammad's son-in-law Ali and his line as the rightful successors to the Prophet. Iran is the only country today where the Shiah predominate. In other Moslem countries the Shiah minority has generally felt excluded or ignored, and resents the Sunni leaders who rule them.

A deep-seated hostility between the Sunnis and the Shiahs exists in Afghanistan, particularly since the bulk of the Shiah minority are concentrated among the Hazarah ethnic group in the central mountains, who have been exploited by the dominant Sunnis. Today the Afghan Shiah have the example of the successful Shiah fundamentalist revolution in Iran to inspire them to seek a religious revolution in their own country—a threat that worries both the government leaders and their Soviet advisers.

Friday is the Moslem holy day, when the men of each community go to the mosque to hear the weekly *khutbah* (sermon). The Afghan mosque is generally a simple building, entered through a long open porch flanked with wood columns. Inside is a large rectangular room with a prayer niche opposite the doors, so arranged that the congregation is facing Mecca. There are no images, no paintings, nothing to distract from concentration on the devotional prayers. Few Afghan mosques have a screened area where women may worship in seclusion, so women generally worship at home.

Islam as formulated by Muhammad is above all a practical religion. Its ideals are attainable, it theology simple. It dispenses with mystical sacraments and priestly hierarchy. Any Moslem male who has the ability, the inclination, and the knowledge of the Koran can assume the role of a religious functionary. As a result the Moslem clergy is an unformalized group. The active religious leaders in Afghanistan are associated with the mosques, of which there may be 15,000, organized into five grades. The imams are in charge of those mosques belonging to the three highest grades. Muezzins attend to those in the fourth grade, and mullahs to those in the fifth. At the top of the Afghan clergy is a loosely knit organization of Moslem clerics called the council of the learned *(jamiyyat-i ulema)*, composed of the most revered religious leaders. This council was created by the government in 1931 to make appointments for posts in many mosques and to verify the religious principles of pending legislation. Its power has been greatly diminished in recent years.

The mullahs make up the bulk of the clergy in Afghanistan. Each mullah is in charge of a village mosque and is supported by community contributions. It is his duty to instruct his congregation in the principles of Islam and to conduct a mosque school *(maktab)*. In thousands of Afghan villages, boys from five to nine years of age receive what is often their only education at the *maktab*. Here they learn passages from the Koran, and a smattering of reading, writing, and arithmetic. There is no standard curriculum, although in villages that do not have a government school, the *maktab* may receive free school materials from the Ministry of Education. Ordinarily the *maktab* is supported by contributions from the students' parents. Girls learn moral lessons from tales of ancestors, saints, and heros. If there is a male member of their extended family who is a religious teacher, as if often the case, they may receive more formal religious instruction at home.

The influence of the mullah is thus very great in the village, for his congregation includes the whole population, and he is often the only available educator. Since the mullah himself is seldom a man of any extensive education, he may be very conservative. He fears that modernizing influences might weaken his authority among his people. Many of the rural parents, particularly the nomads who cling fiercely to their traditional way of life, agree with the conservative mullahs that too much modern education breeds disobedience and discontent among the young people.

The Moslem religion includes a code of law called the *Shariah*, which regulates not only legal decisions but also basic beliefs, religious practices, and social behavior. It teaches man how to behave and act righteously, how to live a life governed by the will of God, and how to conduct his spiritual and temporal affairs. The foundations upon which both Moslem theology and the Shariah were formulated are the Koran, the sayings and acts of Muhammad, the precedents set by Muhammad's companions, and the decisions made continuously over the years by the communities of learned Moslems.

Before the promulgation of the 1964 constitution, the Shariah was the fundamental law of Afghanistan, enforced by the Ministry of Justice. That constitution made the judiciary an independent branch of government and put secular law above religious law for the first time in Afghan history. Conflict between the old and new in the transition period was inevitable, and conservative mullahs led protests and demonstrations against the visible modification of such Moslem customs as polygamy and the veiling of women. The government dealt quietly but firmly with such incidents and considerably curbed the authority of the religious leaders. Many civil and criminal codes based on European models were adopted, and more were being written when the Saur Revolution interrupted the orderly modernization of the country. Fundamentalist religious leaders have played no small role in leading the popular resistance to the left-wing radicals who seized control of the Kabul government.

Bypassing the conservative religious leaders is far easier in Kabul than in the provinces, for the religion of the educated urban dwellers is much more sophisticated than that of the illiterate country people. The tribesman of Afghanistan has an almost fanatical devotion to his religion, but at the same time only a limited knowledge of its tenets. For instance, the Koran strictly forbids any Moslem to kill another who is innocent of offense. Yet blood revenge of family against family when a wrong had been done has always been a rule of tribal law. In most cases the tribesmen are not aware that their revenge violates Shariah.

Alongside his faith in God and in Muhammad as the Messenger of God, the rural Afghan retains a host of local pre-Moslem customs, including a strong belief in the supernatural, in witchcraft, magic, charms, spells, and superstitions. Muhammad's dictum that no super-human being exists apart from God has not obliterated the ghosts, jinns, fairies, demons, and satans whom the country people believe have always controlled much of what happens in the world. To combat their evil influence, there are certain prescribed phrases to repeat, or specific simple rituals like hanging a bit of cloth on a pole by a tomb, or amulets and talismans that are obtained from self-appointed seers who wander about the countryside or attach themselves to some holy spot. Evil spirits are believed responsible for sickness, and disease is commonly treated by a local religious leader or pious layman.

One of the most common sights of the Afghan countryside is the shrine that almost every village has close to its walls, or that may be found along any country road. This may be a mosque or the tomb of a saint, a cairn of stones or a solitary tree, a cave or a spring of water. Such spots are regarded as holy, since the people believe that some saintly person haunts or inhabits them. These shrines may honor biblical or Koranic personages, such as the famous tomb of Ali at Mazar-i-Sharif, or they may commemorate a *pir* (saintly person) whose family still lives in the village. Whoever the person was, the country people believe that his spirit still dwells in his shrine, and the women in particular go there to worship, because their access to the mosque is limited if it has no separate section for them. They bring offerings and special feasts, make pilgrimages and sacrifices at the spot. Vows and contributions are given in the saint's name. In return, the spirit is believed to heal the sick, to give children to barren women, to protect property, and to extend his paternal benevolence over the whole village.

A nurse-midwife, trained by the World Health Organization, makes a home visit to provide postnatal care. Both traditional remedies and modern medicines are used in rural Afghanistan. United Nations/K. Muldoon

The villagers are devout Moslems, but a personal spirit dwelling among them gives them more comfort than a remote and awe-inspiring Allah.

Overlaid on the simple theology of Islam practiced in the villages is the mystic philosophy of Sufism, once quite prevalent among educated Afghans and an aspect of religion that has colored Afghan culture. Over the centuries some Moslems have found the monotonous regularity of the ritual and the simple logic of Moslem theology inadequate to yield spiritual satisfaction. In their desire to know the Supreme Being as a personal God, which impersonal ceremony failed to satisfy, some of these questing individuals formed Sufi orders or brotherhoods. They were not intended to replace orthodoxy, but rather to seek the Supreme Being through personal experience, either through meditation, repeated prayers and chanting, artificial stimulants (including drugs), or violent movement (such as that practiced by the whirling dervishes).

The shrines and places of pilgrimage in Afghanistan attracted such mystics, or Sufis. The orders have practically disappeared today and mysticism is certainly declining, but Sufi meditation still has its intellectual appeal to the educated Afghan.

The influence of Sufism is evident in Afghanistan at two very different levels—in the mystic philosophy and literature of the educated classes, and then in a much different form in the folklore of the common people. All Afghan Sufis expressed themselves in poetry, which broadened their appeal because most literate and nonliterate Afghans, regardless of which language they speak, regard themselves as poets. Talented poets are honored and remembered because poetry is an oral medium that permits universal communication in an immobile society. The ideal personality type was defined in Afghan poetry, as were the ideal relations between individuals, within the group, and with outsiders. All Afghan men think of themselves as bold warriors, an attitude expressed in their folklore.

Sufi mysticism seeped into the unwritten folk literature of the countryside, which was spread by bards and mullahs and passed on orally from generation to generation. The old legends of the eleventh-century *Shahnamah* (Book of Kings) and romantic tales of spiritual and heroic love and valor are taught to Afghan children. Young Afghans learn the deeply mystical Sufi poetry.

One finds the outlook of the people permeated by a remarkable fusion of mystic ideas, saint and spirit worship, fairy tales and ghost stories, heroic songs of battle, romantic poetry, proverbs and wise sayings. This kind of thinking tends to be both emotional and conservative, rather than rational and objective. It causes conflicts in values when the uneducated Afghan comes in contact with modern Western concepts and ideas.

Although the Afghans claim otherwise, the practice of other faiths is not encouraged in Afghanistan. Christian missionaries had worked for years in education and a Christian church was actually built in Kabul in the 1960s, but it was closed and torn down on government orders in the 1970s. Missionary work since then has been strictly confined to assistance in activities like medicine and social work.

CHAPTER IX

Living Patterns

Since 1979 the tensions of war have impinged on daily life in Afghanistan, and any description of what is normal today in city, town, or rural village cannot ignore the ambushes on the highways, attacks on government military posts, sabotage of bridges and dams, bombing of power plants and radio installations, sudden assassinations on city streets, and search-and-destroy missions launched by the military in retaliation. The anger at what has happened to their country is widespread among the Afghans, but the people have paid a heavy price for the willingness of many of their numbers to take up arms against the left-wing government and its Soviet advisers. The technological force that the Soviets supplied and brought to bear against men armed only with portable weapons was awesome. Yet the atmosphere in the countryside is one of determination to resist in every way possible yet another invasion and attempt to impose alien control. The Moslem faith and the Afghan code of honor dictate that submission to an unwelcome and oppressive government is simply unacceptable.

Cities

The cities of Afghanistan grew up where trade routes met and provided access to the outside world. Today main highways link the five principal cities of Afghanistan—Kabul, Kandahar, Herat, Mazar-i-Sharif, and Kunduz.

Before 1978, perhaps 15 percent of the Afghan population lived in those cities. The displacements of guerrilla warfare caused refugees to flock to Kabul, so that its population today is greatly swollen with

Aerial view of the city of Kabul.   United Nations/Sigeloff

A street scene in the heart of Kabul, with a bridge over the Kabul River in the background.
United Nations

transients. This influx badly strains the housing and the urban services that are available, and a great deal of official attention must be directed to preventing unrest and maintaining control over both the normal urban population and the shifting masses of displaced persons.

Urban life in Afghanistan is also in a great state of flux because it was in the cities that the most profound changes were taking place in the patterns of living before the revolution. The educated class—people who have been exposed to and are participating in activities of the modern world—are concentrated there. In the urban population one saw in the 1960s and 1970s a growing distinction among economic classes. Wealth and aristocracy formed a thin upper crust. A middle class was slowly growing, made up of professional men, teachers, government employees, small-industry owners, energetic shopkeepers, and the like. A new group of factory workers and providers of services was also emerging. Among the urban people friendships were being made outside the kin group, and young people were demanding some say in choosing their marriage partners.

The small upper- and middle-class group wielded an inordinate amount of power in the country. From it were drawn the men who ran Afghanistan—its government officials, its development planners and executors, its industrial entrepreneurs, its financiers, it managerial talent, its educators, and the rest. One of the country's gravest problems was that there were not enough capable, educated Afghans to meet its needs.

The numbers have been sadly depleted since the revolution. The members of the royal family and other officials loyal to the royal government were systematically purged by the P.D.P.A. governments or have fled the country to escape being wiped out. In fact, any government officials not willing to join the communist party and swear loyalty to its leaders lost their positions, and those suspected of being in opposition were imprisoned and executed. Military officers faced the same dilemma. There is no accurate record of what proportion of the educated elite of Afghanistan was destroyed by the left-wing governments, but since the P.D.P.A. following was very small and all educated people unwilling to join them came under suspicion, the thousands who were wiped out must have included a substantial segment of the country's trained human resources. Tens of hundreds of Soviet advisers and technicians have been brought in to replace them.

The group that seized control in 1979 came largely from the new middle class, and in spite of the frequent political tension and the constant backdrop of tanks and heavy artillery and soldiers patrolling the streets, the transition to middle-class life goes on in the urban centers. Multistoried buildings, restaurants, general stores, super-markets, and garages change the cityscape. New factories have been built around the cities, and mass housing is gradually being erected for industrial workers. A Russian-built prefab factory manufactures identical structures, which are often erected inside Kabuli compounds as second houses.

Today's Afghan, if he can afford it, seeks some of the material comforts of modern life. Housing in the new urban residential sections, although still hidden behind high walls, is being built with modern conveniences. Here there is running water in taps and electric light (when the power stations are functioning). Consumer items such as cars, radios, refrigerators, books, tools, appliances, and toys are luxuries available to those of means or with political connections.

The most conspicuous change that contact with the outside world has brought to the people in the cities is the gradual conversion to Western dress. As a man prospers, he adds one item of Western clothing after another to his national costume. This gives many of the men on the city streets a curiously hybrid appearance. Full Western dress has been adopted by government officials, professional men, intellectuals, and young men in the colleges and high schools. Karakul caps are worn with Western clothes both outdoors and in public buildings.

Women in the cities for the past twenty years have been emerging from purdah, the custom of secluding women, which in the past required them to wear the *chadri,* the voluminous garment (also known as a *burka*) worn over the women's clothes and faces when outside their homes. Now many upper-class, educated women appear on the streets in Western dress and hold positions in government and industry. Even those women who still appear veiled in the city streets may have abandoned the national costume in favor of European dress.

A tanner smooths out a hide in a shop in Kabul.   United Nations

In the old areas of the cities and in the urban bazaars will be found the traditional Afghans who cling to their ancient ways, contributing sights, sounds, colors, smells, and noises to a mosaic of infinite variety. Here housing is often primitive and makeshift, with few amenities. In the commercial streets, nearly every kind of merchandise imaginable has its own special area—the cattle market in one quarter, the grain merchants in another, elsewhere the endless stalls of fruits and vegetables whose owners keep them fresh by splashing them with water from the ditch in the street. Here is an alley of butchers, with chunks of bloody meat hanging from pegs in the open air. Here are sacks of nuts of a dozen varieties piled along the way, baskets of eggs, trays of sticky homemade candy.

Here the craftsmen of every trade in the country make and sell their wares. The cobblers fashion embroidered sandals and red slippers with pointed toes. The tiny blue flames of the silversmiths are fanned by their bellows from dawn until dusk. Coppersmiths deafen the passersby with the pounding of their hammers on huge trays, pots, and pitchers. Potters shape earthenware bowls and jugs on foot-driven wheels. The fingers of the basket makers fly faster than the eye can follow, and carpenters drop long curls of shavings from hand chisels.

On another street skins and hides hang from pegs or lie in stacks in the narrow shops, beside leather water bags and tangles of harness. Carpets lie along another alley for all to see and feel—cotton and wool strips in bright colors, or the finely tied Herat carpets with their red, white, and black elephant's pad design. Tiny cubbyholes stacked with bolts of cloth line another street—cottons, bright silks, handwoven wool, fine camel's or goat's hair. Beautiful embroidery on cloth and on skins can be found beside excellent handwoven donkey and camel saddlebags and fancy leather vests and sheepskin coats. The tailors are busy taking measurements for the shirts and trousers of the national costume, their foot-pedal sewing machines on the floor in their doorways. Rows of secondhand suits and overcoats and the *chadris* that the veiled women wear hang in grotesque folds.

In the city bazaars, if the Afghan looks long enough, can be found almost anything needed—hawked by vendors, displayed on head trays, strung on wires, draped from rope, heaped on doorsteps, hung on pegs, hidden in corners, dangling from rafters, stacked in doorways, piled on tables, thrown in boxes, dumped under chairs—crowded into an unbelievable confusion in some of the most jam-packed merchant marts of the world.

Towns

The towns of Afghanistan are generally located where several major trails intersect, usually near a large stream. The major towns are all provincial capitals, with Maimana, Baghlan, Pul-i-Khumri, and Jalalabad being more urban than most.

When the royal government introduced a new administrative structure in 1964, the country was divided into twenty-nine provinces, all technically equal in rank. In an effort to speed up economic and political development, it was decided that provincial size should be such that all residents would be able to reach the provincial capital in no more than a day's travel. The towns designated as provincial capitals became the commercial, administrative, and communications centers of the countryside, with lower-grade civil servants and quasimilitary police assigned to each.

Each town also has a bazaar, on a much smaller scale than the urban bazaars, but with the same kinds of artisans making and selling their wares. The villagers and rural people bring farm produce and simple craft work to the town bazaar to sell, using donkeys, horses, or their own backs for transport. Their goods may be used locally or in turn shipped to the cities by truck, camel, or donkey.

Everyone who comes and goes stops at the teahouse *(chaikana)* in the town bazaar to relate or receive the latest local news. A transistor radio there also provides news of the outside world.

The Afghan national dress prevails in the towns and villages, consisting of two basic garments for both men and women. A long, loose-fitting, wide-sleeved shirt, belted with a sash or cartridge belt, is worn over very full trousers, which are gathered and tied at the waist with a string. These trousers taper at the ankle but are astonishingly full at the waist—sometime as wide as eight or ten yards. On very special holidays or among more prosperous people this costume may be white or brightly colored, but more often the shirt and trousers are dull grays or tans or have become drab with age and hard usage. Frequent tears and patches reflect the very modest standard of living of the country.

An Afghan man is almost never seen with his head uncovered. In the country men wear either gray wool caps or long lengths of cotton cloth wound turban fashion around an embroidered skullcap or a bowl-

A street of shops in Kandahar.   United Nations

shaped straw frame, with one end of the turban dangling. The cloth has many uses besides being a head covering. Unrolled it can be used to pull a companion over a wall or to drop a pail down a well. It should be long enough to serve as a shroud, should a man die away from home.

Over their shirt and trousers the men often wear a vest. In cool weather they wind bright wool shawls around head and shoulders or wear padded coats or cloaks. A sheepskin coat *(postin)* is a must in really cold weather. The women seldom seem to add anything to their costume for protection against the cold except warm wool shawls, perhaps because there is little to take them outside their homes in winter. Children dress much like their parents, sometimes with intricate embroidery in bright colors on their shirts. Tiny tots toddle about the courtyards in summer in nothing but a small shirt.

Villages

The residents of the thousands of villages in Afghanistan are farmers, who till small plots of grain and vegetables, tend orchards where water is sufficient, and graze livestock in the less watered areas. Most villages are occupied by kinship groups, and the location of every village was determined by the availability of water and tillable land. If the spot was defensible, so much the better.

The Afghan village clusters closely together in the center of its grain fields and orchards, with the houses built on nonproductive land. A nearby row of poplars or spreading plane trees marks the course of the running stream that is the lifeblood of the village. Here the animals drink, the men bathe and trim their beards and mustaches, the women pound clean their laundry on the rocks. An open ditch of water usually flows from the stream through the village, providing water for the households.

Often the village is surrounded by crumbling fortification walls, built during earlier eras of strife. Near these walls are the cemetery, the threshing floors, and often a shrine, the tomb of a revered mullah or local *pir*. This spot is sheltered by a lofty tree and marked by a cluster of tall poles hung with flags, ribbons, and strips of cloth tied there by village women who have sought an answer to a prayer from the holy spirit dwelling there.

An unpaved street runs through the center of the village. Here is found the mosque and a teahouse or two, and often a village well. The colorful bazaars of the towns are missing because there are few full-time artisans living in the villages. Instead the residents go to the nearest town to sell their agricultural goods and to obtain the few essentials that they do not produce themselves—tea, salt, cloth, mirrors, tools, lamps, kerosene, matches, and the like. Itinerant peddlers may also provide these necessities.

Transport in the villages has traditionally been on foot or by horse, donkey, or camel. Only since World War II have bicycles become a part of the village scene.

The simple flat-roofed dwellings are in small gardens behind high blank walls fronting on the village lane. A rich man still builds one or more watchtowers on his house as a sign of wealth, and these were put to use once again by the resistance in the 1980s. Because the towers are high and cool in summer, they also serve as sleeping rooms. Within the compound will be a place for livestock, a small pool for household uses, a cooking oven, and perhaps a crude latrine.

The house is built of sun-baked mud brick, the roof of reed matting plastered with clay. (It must be remudded every fall to keep it from leaking, and shoveled free of snow in the winter to prevent it from collapsing.) The house was constructed by the men of the family with the help of their neighbors, who received their meals in return. The villagers work together building roads, bridges, houses, irrigation ditches, and canals—a reflection of a sense of community based on strong kinship ties.

In western Afghanistan the ordinary square village dwellings have dome-shaped roofs, with an opening to admit air and light and expel smoke. As the family expands, another beehive hut is simply added to the interconnected village. In the mountain villages stone replaces mud brick as the building material.

The family lives in one main room, with sometimes a cool cellar beneath for storing food and escaping from the summer heat. On the floor are simple woven rugs of cotton and wool made by local craftsmen. The family sleeps on the floor, or on the roof in summer, on homemade cotton mattresses that are spread out at night. A carved or painted chest or two hold household possessions, but there will be little other furniture except perhaps a grain bin and a samovar.

The more prosperous families will have a reception room at the front, and perhaps a women's section *(harem)* and court at the back. Heating is seldom adequate, since all types of fuel are scarce and expensive and there is no way of heating the whole house. Families keep warm in the winter by gathering closely about a charcoal brazier *(sandali)*, which is placed on the floor with a table or frame about two feet above it. All the family quilts are draped over it to form a circle some three or four yards across. At night, when it is often bitterly cold, the family sleeps as tightly as possible within the circle where the heat is contained, with only their heads exposed to the cold air of the room.

The people of the village elect two officials to carry on the village administration. The *malik*, who is generally head of the most important family in the village, holds a position comparable to a mayor and is responsible for collecting taxes, settling disputes, and seeing that justice is administered. He entertains official guests. The *malik* serves without salary and is rewarded in the high respect accorded him by the villagers. The other important village official is the *marib*, who distributes the irrigation water of the village.

Nomads

Between two and three million of Afghanistan's people are nomadic, depending principally on livestock for their living. Most of them are Pushtuns, Kirghiz, or Baluch (an ethnic group that predominates across the southern border in Pakistan). Their sheep and goats furnish meat and dairy products to eat, wool for clothing and rugs, and goat hair for tent fabric. The nomads often barter these items with farmers for grain, vegetables, fruit, and nuts.

A family of nomads moving to a new location.   UN Photo 153845/Kate Bader

A family of nomad camps by a lake in the Hindu Kush.   United Nations/Sigeloff

Some groups are semisedentary, with landholdings where part of the clan lives year-round and tends seasonal crops, while designated members of the group travel with their flocks in the summer to higher elevations and stay there as long as grass is available for grazing. Other groups are completely nomadic, moving with the seasons from highland pastures in the summer to lowlands in the winters. They own no land, but have traditional grazing privileges over specific areas, which they defend fiercely against all intruders.

The distances they travel are impressive. Before 1961 several thousand nomads known in Pakistan as *powindahs (povindars)*, whom the Afghans call *Kuchis (Kochis)*, used to come down from the southern Afghan highlands and cross the border into Pakistan, spreading out over the North-West Frontier area and beyond. This migration had occurred for centuries, and when a dispute with Pakistan in the fall of 1961 closed the border, the interruption of the traditional migration pattern caused severe economic hardship. The tribes actually fought with each other as they competed for new winter pasture within Afghanistan, and the government provided airdrops of forage for the flocks.

Now the internal migration patterns have become routine, and every spring and fall season finds the roads and pack trails ajangle with the bells of the camels, donkeys, black goats, and sheep of the nomads. The women are wrapped in black shawls, and some of them wear bright red or blue trousers to distinguish them from their men so they will not be shot by mistake during tribal raiding. Heavy silver bracelets on wrists and ankles and ornamental bands of silver coins sewed to their brightly embroidered blouses give them a gypsylike appearance. The men, each with a rifle slung over his shoulder and a knife in his belt, are tall and savage appearing in their dark garments and large turbans above hawk-like brown eyes and bristling mustaches. They drive their flocks before them with the help of fierce, deep-chested dogs, whose ears are cropped so wild animals cannot get hold of them. These are watchdogs rather than pets, and are greatly feared by all save their owners. The camels and donkeys are laden with a fantastic variety of bundles—tents and tent frames, layers of sleeping mats, bales of hides or of rough-hewn wood being brought down for trading, cooking pots and utensils, sacks of provisions, sticks and dried dung for cooking fuel, and very frequently live fowl, a newborn kid, or a stoic baby strapped atop the animal's load.

They travel in the cool of the morning and evening, pitching camp beside a running stream during the heat of the day. The flocks drink, and graze what scant grass can be found among the stony terrain. The men unload the animals and pitch the tents. The women carry water, gather fuel, and set up a campfire, and soon a huge pot of soup or rice cooked with tiny chunks of meat or vegetables will be surrounded by the family circle, each dipping in the fingers of his right hand to eat.

Many of the nomads are both stockbreeders and traders, seeking markets for their wool and hides and carrying the simple necessities of daily life with them to barter with the country farmers along their migration routes. A few are wealthy moneylenders who finance seed and tools and other obligations, keeping the farmers perpetually in their debt. The improvement in the economic status of many nomads is visible in the trucks they now use to transport their baggage, women, children, and elderly folk.

The Moslem faith and the obligations of kinship shape daily life among the nomads more than any other part of the Afghan population because of the nature of their living patterns. For nomadic people, total social and economic cooperation are crucial to survival, reinforcing the importance of the family or clan as the governing structure of their lives. A reciprocal set of rights and obligations determines each individual's relation to others in his group and outside his group. Friendships are formed within the kin group, and marriages take place within it (with a first cousin being the preferred mate). Social security and welfare are provided by the clan, and it will continue that way until progressive development programs make kinship support less crucial to the rural people.

Central government officials in Kabul are very aware of how little control they have over the nomads, and have for several decades sought to settle them on newly irrigated land where they will be much easier to supervise. What the bureaucrats cannot combat is the high value nomads place on their independence and their disdain for any authority other than their own tribal leadership. They look down on the village farmers, considering themselves superior beings. Only if they lose their flocks, which are their livelihood, will they settle down on the land.

Their viewpoint is completely inward looking, and they simply do not see the world from the same perspective as the outward-looking government officials who plan development programs. When the nomads are contemptuous of the Kabul government, they simply ignore its existence, and as long as they travel off the main highways, there is not a great deal the government can do about it.

The irrigation projects financed by the government have had an indirect effect on the nomads, however, in that they impinge on the traditional grazing lands. When the nomads return from summer pastures, they may find part of their winter pasture occupied by pioneering farmers. The government backs the farmers in any disputes, and many nomads have found that the best solution is to become seminomadic and settle on the grasslands of their winter quarters in order to retain them.

Social Patterns

Life in the rural villages and nomad camps is so circumscribed compared to that in the towns and cities of Afghanistan that the outlook of the rural farmer and herdsman is very alien to that of the urban dweller. The young people who attend school in the towns and cities are lifted out of the narrow confines of concrete experience that limit the horizons of the illiterate farmer and learn new skills along with the concepts and ideas of the larger world. Education becomes the key that unlocks the door to important changes in status, both for the young men who will assume leadership roles, and for the young women who acquire skills that permit them to lead lives more of their own choosing.

An understanding of the kinds of opportunities open to the Afghans requires a discussion of the patterns of family life and the status of women, as well as an explanation of the scope and kind of education available, who receives it, and what effect it has on national life.

Rural Family Social Organization

Society in rural Afghanistan (and most of Afghanistan is rural) is organized in family and tribal units. The Afghan family includes the head of the family, his wife or wives, his unmarried children, his married sons and their wives and children. All family members, young and old, are regarded as the common responsibility of the entire family. As a result beggars are rare in Afghanistan, for the aged, the sick, the handicapped, and the unemployed are cared for by the family as a matter of course.

The eldest male, as head of the family, has complete authority over his entire household. The position of family patriarch generally passes to the eldest son. Sons stay in their fathers' households, while married daughters go to their husbands' families. There is preference for marriages within the extended family or among near relatives.

In this type of family most property is owned jointly, and the entire family's earnings are pooled and distributed by the patriarch. When the head of the family dies, the property is divided among the sons to keep the family from becoming too large. The eldest son remains in the patriarchal dwelling.

Each married couple among settled peoples has a room or small house in a group of flat-roofed, mud-brick houses within a high mud-walled compound. The nomads follow a similar family living arrangement. In the summer months when pasture grass grows high on the mountains, they pitch an encampment of handwoven black goat's-hair tents thrown over rectangular frames of rough poles. The parents and unmarried children live in one tent. A Moslem may have more than one wife, and each has her tent. The women of the family weave a tent for each son when he marries. In the winter they move to the lower valleys to escape the snows, and a number of related families set up their tents together in a larger camp.

The family unit, called *khanadan* (in Pushtu) is the smallest in the tribal structure. Closely related families join together to form a clan. The clan joins with other clans to form a subtribe, called *kheyl*.

The leader of the tribe is the khan, usually a member of the most aristocratic family group in the tribe, the *khan kheyl*. The khan is responsible for the protection and prosperity of his people, as well as for settling disputes and carrying out decisions of the *jirgah*, or tribal assembly. Like the malik in a village, he is held in high regard by his kinsmen—respected for his qualities of leadership, wisdom, piety, valor, and hospitality. Learning and renowned ancestry are also important.

Many tribes have a hereditary chieftainship. In other tribes the men are very independent and exercise their right to settle all important issues, including who shall lead the tribe, in a tribal council (*jirgah*). The tribesmen come together whenever necessary in a *jirgah* to discuss, in town-meeting fashion, their current concerns. They do not vote formally, but through discussion and debate gradually reach a consensus, which is formally acclaimed as the will of the tribe.

Living in this tribal milieu focuses the Afghan's values within his kin group. His personal honor and prestige are all-important to him. To cite an example, a shepherd tending his flocks might be set upon by robbers wanting his sheep. Although obviously outnumbered, he will fight to protect his land and his animals, even though he might be killed in the encounter. He could never face his family with pride again if he failed to defend what was rightfully his. This same determination to defend what is rightfully theirs inspires the *mujahidin* to continue their guerrilla warfare against the communist government and the Soviet military, particularly after members of their families have been killed or driven out of their villages and across the border.

His particular values give purpose to the rural Afghan's rugged and generally dangerous way of life—a life devoid of almost every material comfort. The narrow prestige and honor he holds so dear have become meaningful goals for his existence. Custom, tradition, and centuries of struggling to survive have instilled in him the unshakable belief that this way of life is right and proper.

On the other hand, the difficulties of life between mountain, desert, and invader have not robbed the tribesman of his belief in the dignity and equality of the individual. In fact, his pastoral existence has made the tribesman a determined democrat. The Afghan is a fiercely proud individual, and there are few barriers of class in his society. The tribesman meets his chief on an equal footing, the tenant has access to his landlord, the servant to his master, and the officials running the government in Kabul are supposed to be first among equals. If they are not respected or their ways run counter to tribal traditions, their laws are simply ignored.

Rural Women

The rural women of Afghanistan have not shared the independence of their men because of the strong religious sanction that has been given to purdah, the custom of secluding women. The Moslem religion has always placed women in a position subordinate to men, a situation that prevails in Moslem countries until education is made available to women. In Afghanistan the rules of purdah enforced the isolation of all Afghan women from any men except their immediate male relatives, until a tremendous social revolution was undertaken in 1959. Then the

An Afghan mother brings her child to a rural health clinic.   United Nations/K. Muldoon

first steps were taken to free Afghan women from the *chadri*.

In the past, when a young girl reached the age of puberty, she entered purdah, which required her to wear a *chadri* whenever she left the family compound. The country women have never worn the *chadri* to the universal extent that their urban sisters did, since they must often work beside their husbands in the fields. Their seclusion has, however, been just as strict, in that they should not meet or talk with any men who are not members of the family. Their custom is either to run and hide when they see a nonrelated man approaching; if that is not possible, they wrap the long scarf that is part of their costume over their heads and turn their backs. Only the nomad women ignore the purdah rules and go about their activities without concealing themselves from the male half of the population.

There is only a vague reference to purdah in the Koran. It is a custom that existed in the Middle East even before Islam, and probably originated in the days when aggressive men stole women. Husbands and fathers kept their women locked behind the family walls in those times because they were valuable economic assets. Chastity was highly regarded, wives cost money, daughters commanded a bride price, and marriages were often the means to favorable political alliances. The protective function of purdah is rapidly disappearing in modern society, but the custom is curiously enough taking on a status role. Village men who have achieved some economic success may insist that their wives observe purdah to indicate that they no longer have to do fieldwork or contribute to the family's livelihood.

Although the revolutionary government in 1978 decreed a minimum age for marriage, prohibited arranged marriages, and outlawed the payment of bride price, marriage arrangements among rural families are still negotiated by the two families concerned. This does not mean,

---

Extract from the Koran, Chapter 4, on the superiority of men over women:

4:34   Men have authority over women because Allah has made the one superior to the others, and because they spend their wealth to maintain them. Good women are obedient. They guard their unseen parts because Allah has guarded them.

Translation from Arabic to English by N. J. Dawood (New York: Penguin Books, 1956)

however, that young people are strangers when they marry, for the parents prefer a mate from within the related family. Thus the bride and groom are very often cousins and have known each other from childhood. The boy is usually between eighteen and twenty, the girl sixteen to eighteen at the time of their marriage.

Once the two families have agreed on a suitable match, the marriage settlement is negotiated. The groom's family customarily pays a bride price to the girl's family—usually money or livestock, or both—which validates the marriage contract. The bride price remains with the bride's family, and serves to both compensate the family for its loss of a productive resource and as a sort of prepaid support payment in case the husband seeks a divorce and the girl must return to her family.

An elaborate engagement ceremony follows the settling of these details, and the groom's family pays a formal visit to the bride's family to set the wedding date. The groom's mother brings gifts of clothes and jewels for the bride, who receives a dowry from her own family—clothing, bedding, and the other household utensils the couple will need in the early years of their marriage. The wedding itself is marked by three days of prenuptial ceremonies, with all the near relatives gathering for the festivities, and music, entertainment, and food provided for all. After the Moslem ceremony unites the couple, there is a joyous procession to the groom's home.

Islam permits a man to have four wives. In actual practice, however, few Afghans can afford to pay the bride price for more than one. Abandonment of polygamy was encouraged by the royal family and by the example of the former king and queen. Islam requires that girls be virgins at the time of their marriage and remain faithful to their husbands throughout their lives—the penalty for adultery among the tribes being death.

The subordinate position of rural women to their husbands does not

Extract from the Koran, Chapter 4, on women and marriage:

4:2   Give orphans the property which belongs to them. Do not exchange their valuables for worthless things or cheat them of their possessions; for this would surely be a great sin. If you fear that you cannot treat orphans [orphan girls] with fairness, then you may marry other women who seem good to you: two, three, or four of them. But if you fear that you cannot maintain equality among them, marry one only or any slave-girls you may own. This will make it easier for you to avoid injustice.

Translation from Arabic to English by N. J. Dawood (New York: Penguin Books, 1956)

deprive wives of the status appropriate to their husbands' positions. The wife of the family patriarch manages the household, directing the activities of her daughters-in-law and controlling the larder. The wives in each generation have their voice in family affairs and exert considerable influence on their husbands' decisions. They have a major say in decisions to abandon their homes in the face of war, and assumed almost complete responsibility for their families in the refugee camps outside the country, because most of their men returned to Afghanistan to fight. These country women of Afghanistan are a strong, sturdy breed, accustomed to carrying the water and firewood and turning their hand to the plow if need be. The tribal women have often been required to face dangerous situations courageously. There are few of them who do not know how to handle guns and ammunition, and they frequently serve as spies and messengers for the resistance.

Islamic divorce sounds so simple as to be astonishing to Westerners.

The husband has only to say three times to his wife in the presence of witnesses, "I divorce you," and the deed is done. A woman can go before a judge and give cause to be granted a divorce—generally cruelty, sterility, or repeated adultery. Marriage termination is, however, not very common. Not only are there strong social pressures against divorce, but a man usually considers carefully whether he can afford to dispense with his wife before he takes such an important step, and a woman has to convince her family that she has good cause to return to the paternal household. (Afghanistan is not yet ready to permit her to establish her own home alone.)

Inheritance laws generally pertain to the distribution of the family property among the sons, since the daughters have received their shares as dowries when they married. There are set customs to assure a widow of a livelihood if she loses her husband. She inherits a share of his property, and she is assured of a home and maintenance by her husband's family. In fact, she often marries her late husband's younger brother or some other near relative if she wishes. In any case, she has her place in the household as long as she lives. She will train her daughters in any special skills she may possess, and at her death pass on her personal clothing and jewelry to them.

Rural Education

In spite of the fact that most Afghans can speak two languages, only a small proportion of them can read and write. Not more than 10 percent of the people are literate, and limited educational opportunities keep the bulk of the population from escaping rural poverty. In many rural villages, the only schooling available for children is very scanty religious training by the local mullah.

In an effort to expand the horizons of the rural people, the government broadcasts adult education programs over radio and television, with transistor radios and loudspeakers provided to rural towns and villages by the government. Literacy courses for adults were started under the Five Year Plans, and by 1986 the Afghan government claimed it had enrolled more than a million people. Western observers say, however, that the number was greatly overinflated and that the courses consisted mainly of propaganda and slogans and had little impact on literacy.

The United Nations technical assistance program has been assisting rural community development efforts in Afghanistan for more than thirty years. U.N. experts have established village programs in health, agriculture, education, crafts, social welfare, and training for village instructors and community leaders.

A rural development department in the Ministry of Interior sponsors the program. Initially the emphasis was on self-help in building primary and village schools, in starting literacy courses, in establishing social welfare centers and youth clubs. Demonstrations in agriculture emphasized increased production of poultry and dairy products, vegetables, and fruits for both home consumption and market sale.

These kinds of programs teach illiterate villagers to use modern implements and techniques of farming and improved seed and plants. Veterinarians inoculate animals against disease and teach improved livestock breeding. Health care centers are established in the villages and vaccination programs undertaken. Courses, lectures, films, and demonstrations explain sanitation, health, and child welfare, while village development workers assist in digging latrines and wells. Cottage industries are encouraged, beginning with canning, carpet weaving, and carpentry, and including other skills such as pottery, tanning, shoemaking, masonry, and lapidary where appropriate. Before the war, students of primary teachers' training schools spent two months of their training at a rural development project.

The United Nations Development Program still provides assistance to the Afghan government, but unfortunately, these kinds of activities cannot be effectively carried on when the government controls only the main cities and highways, while war rages in the rural countryside. Only slender beginnings have been made in reaching the many rural people who need such help; but it is this kind of education, aimed at providing the country people with the tools and skills with which to improve their daily life, that will be greatly needed in the months and years to come.

Formal Education

The 1964 constitution stated that education for all Afghan children should be compulsory and free of charge from elementary school through university. As must be expected in a country that has only recently opened up to the outside world, formal education is limited by inadequate school buildings, laboratories, libraries, and teaching materials, and by a shortage of well-trained, adequately paid teachers.

Since World War II the government has been allocating nearly 10 percent of its yearly budget to education. Government plans published in 1983 (the last available) indicated that over 1.7 million students were to be enrolled in 1983 (about 35 percent of the children of school age), compared with 500,000 in 1970. Whether this goal was achieved in the midst of war is impossible to determine.

Formal education is divided into three levels: elementary and secondary (totaling ten years, after the Soviet model), and university, and enrolls about five times as many boys as girls.

Since the Saur Revolution, education has been completely under Soviet control. Soviet advisers run the Ministry of Education. Afghan elementary teachers use a Soviet-style curriculum, teach from new textbooks preaching communism, and are required to attend indoctrination seminars. About a third of the curriculum is now devoted to the study of scientific socialism, dialectical materialism, and a rewritten history of Afghanistan that glorifies the communist regime and its struggle against imperialism. Local teachers are assisted by hundreds of Soviet teachers and instructors. Soviet professors made up perhaps four fifths of the faculty of Kabul University. Thousands of the brightest Afghan students were removed from the secondary schools and the university, often without their parents' consent, and were sent to study in the Soviet Union, especially in the Central Asian republics. The goal was to convert enough young people to the communist cause to lead the next generation of Afghans down the socialist path. This policy will continue as long as the communist government maintains its control and Soviet advisers remain in place.

Almost all towns (provincial capitals) have government elementary schools for at least the first four grades. The quality of the teaching is often very spotty because few school graduates want to go to rural areas to teach. Before the revolution foreign volunteers like members of the U.S. Peace Corps met some of the need. After the revolution the communist party started assigning many of its young recruits to that task—often to their chagrin. Their presence in the towns does, however, provide a network of support for the party and an important means of recruiting more young people to back the government's programs.

In the government's primary schools children are taught Pushtu, Persian, arithmetic, the geography of Afghanistan, and practical training in agriculture and cottage industries. Girls learn needlework, knitting, child care, cooking, and the preliminaries of home economics.

Transition in Urban Areas

Education is, of course, the key to modernization. In Afghanistan secondary schools are found only in large towns and cities, and the young people who complete the curriculum will have the opportunity when they graduate to participate in the commercial and professional activities of the urban areas. Secondary education is free, with the government supplying textbooks and materials, and the number of schools has increased steadily since World War II.

Secondary instruction is divided into intermediate (junior high) and high school (senior high). The curriculum includes Persian, Pushtu, mathematics, history, drawing, chemistry, physics, biology, geology, Arabic, Russian, economics, geography, and physical education. (During the Soviet occupation much of the school day, in both primary and secondary schools, was spent on communist ideology.) The oldest high school in Kabul is Habibia College, which on its establishment in 1904 introduced modern secondary education into Afghanistan. It used to teach English as its major foreign language, as did all other secondary schools except Istiqlal, which taught French, and Mijat, which taught German. Russian has replaced English as the required foreign language in the high schools, and French and West German assistance in educational programs was terminated in 1985.

The first schools for girls were established in 1922. Following their primary and intermediate education young women can choose to go to a high school as preparation for the university, to home economics schools, to nursing and midwifery schools, or to teachers' training schools (which train primary school teachers) for their high school years. Coeducation began in 1958 in the experimental elementary schools associated with the work of a Teachers College of Columbia University team.

Boys finishing intermediate schools often select one of the forty-two vocational schools, which now have Soviet teachers and advisers. There young men receive training in arts and crafts, trade, agriculture, pharmacy, dentistry, technology, and communist ideology. A Department of

Vocational Education was organized in the Ministry of Education in 1947, and new vocational schools were built in the major cities. These vocational schools included teachers' training schools, which were established in all the major provinces and are now all controlled by Soviet advisers.

Students going on to higher education in Afghanistan attend Kabul University (called Kabul Puhantun), which was established in 1946. All faculties are coeducational, and female enrollment in the 1980s ex-

A young woman in Kabul who has abandoned purdah *walks with older members of her family who still wear the* chadri.   United Nations

ceeded male because men were either in the military, had joined the
resistance, or had fled the country. Tuition is free, with the government
supplying instructional materials, clothing, and room and board where
possible. A new modern campus was completed in 1964, bringing all
the university departments together in one place. Construction of the
university buildings was one of the major aid projects of the United
States Agency for International Development (USAID), with assistance
also given for improvement of university administration.

Bachelors' degrees are awarded at Kabul University by faculties of
law and political science, science (mathematics and physics, chemistry
and biology, geology and minerology), literature, religious studies, agriculture, economics, pharmacy, and home economics. All college departments used to include courses in "Principles of Marxist-Leninism,"
"Political Economy," "Dialectical and Historical Materialism," and
"History of the Party." The faculty of medicine, which graduates M.D.s,
as well as a medical school at the Nangarhar University in Jalalabad,
have been amalgamated into a new State Institute of Medicine, which
is tied closely to the Tajik State Medical Institute in the U.S.S.R. Total
enrollment in Kabul University, the Kabul Polytechnic, and Nangarhar
University was officially listed at 12,200 in 1983, down from 20,000
in 1978. Western observers reported that the disruptions of the war
actually decreased enrollments to less than half that number.

At the Institute of Education, part of Kabul University, an improved
program of teacher education was developed in the 1950s and 1960s
under the guidance of Teachers College of Columbia University specialists, with USAID furnishing books, equipment, and scholarships for
Afghan students to study in the United States. (All teacher training
programs were transferred to Soviet control.) The University of Wyo-
ming assisted the faculty of agriculture. Several universities helped the
engineering faculty, which was closed in 1985 to force all engineering

students to attend the Soviet-built Polytechnic Institute. France extended assistance to law and medicine; West Germany to science and economics; Egypt to theology. All aid from noncommunist countries was terminated by the communist governments.

The Soviet Union entered the Afghan education scene in 1965 by providing financing and teachers for vocational training in engineering, petroleum refining, communications, construction, and mining. The role of Soviet advisers greatly increased in the 1970s under President Daud, and during his tenure the university student bodies were greatly politicized by left-wing radicals. Student demonstrations and strikes played an important part in the unrest that led Daud to crack down on the P.D.P.A. leaders, and there were periods when political agitation took precedence over classroom sessions.

The yeasty fermentation that spread through the university campus in the 1970s was controlled by arrests and imprisonments, and demonstrations by both college and high school students, including angry young women, ended in bloodshed when police and army troops opened fire. Participation by students in resistance activities was ended by the communists, and admission of men to university requires completion of three years of military service, or participation in either party work and secret police or civilian military academies.

The Changing Role of Urban Women

Improving the status of women is one of the keys to economic change in Afghanistan. In order to carry out its development plans, Afghanistan has needed more and more educated people. Jobs go begging in government offices for lack of qualified personnel. Nearly all household servants are men. There are many areas in which women could move into the working force and free large numbers of men to expand the needed labor supply. Today teaching is the most popular occupation for Afghan women, with medicine and nursing second—and extremely important in a nation where many women refuse to consult male doctors and nurses. Educated women have also found niches in broadcasting and journalism, in advertising and tourism, and as secretaries, bank clerks, and factory workers. About one of every eight industrial workers is female.

In order for women to join the work force, of course, they must be freed of the restrictions of the *chadri*, which makes it difficult to see or to move about freely. Those who have been through school have already abandoned the veil. Uneducated urban women still generally observe purdah, particularly in provincial towns, but more numerous schools will gradually change this.

The first unsuccessful attempt to get women to discard their *chadris* was made in the 1920s by King Amanullah, who issued royal decrees abolishing purdah. The attempt failed then because the king did not have the support of the religious leaders, or of the army, or of an educated class to endorse progressive social reforms. Even today the abandoning of purdah may not have the support of the mullahs or of certain ultraconservative families, but the change was carefully planned and executed in the fifties by King Zahir to avoid the kind of opposition Amanullah encountered.

A number of preliminary moves paved the way. In the late 1950s Radio Kabul began using women singers and announcers. In 1958 the first delegation of Afghan women attended a conference of Asian women in Ceylon. In 1959 women were sent to the United Nations with the Afghan delegation and to the Afghan Embassy in Washington.

In the spring of 1959 about ten women of high-ranking Kabul families started work as receptionists and hostesses for Ariana Afghan Airlines. A few weeks later a class of girls finishing the sixth grade were offered positions in the Kabul china factory. Forty girls obtained their parents' permission and went to work alongside the men in the factory with only the mildest of protests raised. Unveiled women were also employed by the telephone exchange.

The climax occurred in August 1959, when Prime Minister Daud called in his army generals to tell them that the royal family wished to abolish the *chadri*, and asked their support. He planned that during the August festival of *Jashn* (the Afghan independence celebration) members of the royal family, the cabinet, and high-ranking army officers would appear at the official functions accompanied by their unveiled wives. This would indicate official approval of the innovation, but would not necessitate official action. The *Jashn* crowds, which included representatives from all over Afghanistan, were enthusiastic about the move.

Today urban upper-class women seldom wear the *chadri*, although this could change if fundamentalist Moslems gain control of the government. Education for girls beyond primary school now makes it possible for them to avoid purdah altogether. Thus more and more women are seen in the cities attending official functions, going to movies and restaurants, or at work in offices and factories. The first woman cabinet secretary was Minister of Public Health from 1963 to 1969. Four women deputies were elected to the lower house of Parliament under the 1964 constitution, and one woman was appointed to the upper house in both 1965 and 1969. President Daud appointed a number of women to high positions in his cabinet and government.

The Revolutionary Council that governed Afghanistan after 1978 had a woman member, but women were less prominent in other important government positions, perhaps because they would be targets for the resistance. Their numbers were greater at the middle and lower levels, and their salaries were improved under the communists. Women also performed noncombat-related duties in the military.

The literate urban woman in Afghanistan has much more to say about the choice of a mate and divorce than in the past, although she still must gain the approval of her closest male relatives for both. Her dowry will include a refrigerator, electric range, washing machine, and other modern amenities—material possessions that are beyond the reach of most Afghans.

Cultural Patterns

Modernization should not require the abandonment of the customs and traditions and values that have given meaning to a people's existence throughout remembered history. Whatever degree of success left-wing leaders might achieve in replacing traditional with progressive ways, they could never succeed in homogenizing as diverse and colorful a populace as that of Afghanistan. The culture and customs of the country have not been formed by accident, but rather as a logical response to the turmoil, isolation, and poverty that the Afghans have endured for so many centuries. The resilience and toughness that have resulted have been balanced by deep family ties, universal hospitality, and great enthusiasm for feasts, celebrations, festivals, and folklore. Material possessions have never eased their lives, but the Afghans have established patterns in their daily activities that give vitality and color to their simple villages among the mountain folds and across the desert plains.

Daily Bread

Although many Afghans live on a very slim diet, particularly during the winter months when their gardens are bare, people seem to accept whatever is available. When wheat runs out, barley and dried mulberries are ground into meal for bread. When one crop fails, a substitute is found. The ordinary Afghan diet might seem monotonous, but it is an accepted part of life.

Round flat loaves of unleavened wheat bread are so much a staple in the diet of the rural people of Afghanistan that the word for bread and meal are the same—*nan*. Food grains are among Afghanistan's principal crops, so that bread and rice are mainstays throughout the land. Soup, tea, vegetables, and fruits supplement the low-income family diets. Most vegetables grow locally, principally onions, cabbage, eggplants, turnips, cucumbers, and rhubarb. Excellent fruits—quinces, apples, peaches, apricots, pears, mulberries, cherries, citrus, figs—are available in season, and the Afghan melons and grapes are famous. The vines of the latter grow on mud walls rather than on expensive fences, and the grapes are transported from the vineyards packed in cotton and clay. Raisins and nuts were a traveler's snack food in Afghanistan long before "trail mix" was invented.

In the towns and cities the more prosperous people regularly eat pilau (rice cooked with meat, vegetables, fat called *roghan*, and spices) and a variety of sauces. *Kabab* (cubes of meat roasted on skewers) and fried foods are also favorites—fried chicken, fried eggs, fried pastries filled with meat or vegetables. *Khormah* (lamb fried with potatoes or vegetables) is a well-known Afghan dish. The diet among the wealthier people

includes dried fruit, candy, and sherbets. A large feast will consist of a dozen or more dishes, all of which must be tasted by each guest. Such feasting as a demonstration of generous hospitality is one of the few acceptable ways of showing wealth in Afghanistan.

Meat dishes on the regular menu are a sign of wealth, for the poor people eat meat infrequently and rely on eggs from their own chickens for protein. Mutton, the meat from sheep, is much preferred to beef. All pork products are forbidden by religious precepts. There are certain traditional Moslem rituals for butchering animals, so the villagers still generally purchase them live for slaughter at home. Goat's milk is given to children, but adults prefer their dairy products in the form of yogurt or cheese. The first milk and ice-cream factory was established in Kabul in the early 1970s, and an American-style supermarket has operated since 1965. Only wealthy homes have refrigerators, however. In other households perishable foods must be eaten immediately, or given to neighbors or the poor. Meats, fruits, and vegetables are dried and kept, along with staples such as wheat flour and rice, in cool storerooms.

Drinking tea, brewed strong and heavily sweetened, is a national custom associated with the hospitality always shown to any guest. One cannot enter an Afghan home or place of business without being offered tea or a fruit drink of some kind. The teahouse, be it only a thatch roof on four posts, is the male gathering spot at every village or country crossroads. Here the brass samovar is always hot, and the men sit on string bedframes smoking their water pipes, exchanging the latest news of the neighborhood, and indulging in their love of good fellowship. Because they are Moslems, the Afghans do not drink alcohol.

In normal circumstances, a balanced diet is available in most parts

A government agricultural instructor examines a cauliflower with a group of farmers at an experimental farm in Kunar Province. United Nations/Photo by Ray Witlin

of the country, so that poor health is caused either by poverty or by lack of sanitation rather than by a lack of foodstuffs. Recent years in Afghanistan have, however, been far from normal. The resistance groups, which carried on guerrilla warfare against the Afghan and Soviet armies, operated in most parts of the country. In retaliation for their attacks, the military resorted to mass bombing and strafing to drive out inhabitants of villages that supported the resistance, detroying their houses, orchards, flocks, and irrigation systems so that they would not return. This deprived the *mujahidin* of the food and shelter they needed to carry on their struggle. Particularly in the border areas great stretches of Afghanistan's once-prosperous farmland were laid waste and between four and five million refugees driven from their homes, most of them across the borders into Pakistan and Iran. Increased rural poverty and hunger are the inevitable result.

Health

Afghan adults are on the whole healthy and tough—not surprising when one considers that they have survived a high infant mortality rate, almost complete lack of sanitary facilities, and consistently unhygienic practices all their lives. Impure water in open pools and ditches and the absence of any kind of waste disposal combine to present formidable health hazards. Fortunately, the sun and dry mountain air discourage the growth of bacteria.

The central government has established hospitals and clinics in the main cities of the country, but very limited health care is available in rural areas. In the villages where there are no doctors, people rely on their mullahs to treat them with charms and incantations, or on self-trained *taribs* (traditional, oriental-style physicians) who use herbs, witchcraft, and ancient spells. Village barbers serve as dentists. Midwives assist at childbirth.

Rural attitudes toward disease, deformity, and death are based on a deep-seated Moslem belief that all afflictions are from God. The handicapped are cared for as a matter of course, and individuals with mental peculiarities may develop skills in religious meditation or healing and become important members of their communities.

Folk Art

In keeping with the predominantly rural patterns of life, the artistic expression of the common people is found in their handicrafts, particularly in handweaving and fine carpet design, and in the traditional folk arts of song and dance.

In every town one finds the traditional craft industries—hand milling of grain, woodworking, leatherworking, pottery making, and tile molding. Metalwork is done in small shops throughout the country, using imported sheets of iron. Ironworkers make the local agricultural implements such as plows, spades, pickaxes, as well as knives and utensils. Coppersmiths fashion pots and pans, trays, and jugs. Particularly intricate and beautifully patterned copperware is produced in the northeast and in Kandahar.

Other areas have specialists in handicrafts for which they are noted. The best carpets are made in Dalatabad in the northwest, using wool and dyes prepared locally, while those from Herat are also well known. Both wool and cotton cloth of fine texture are hand woven, and silk weaving is also a specialty. Sheepskin coats of good quality are made at Ghazni, while other areas produce felt furnishings for the yurts of the northern plains. Silversmiths and goldsmiths all over the country have done lapidary work for centuries. Output in the handicraft industries is probably three or four times that of factory-scale industry.

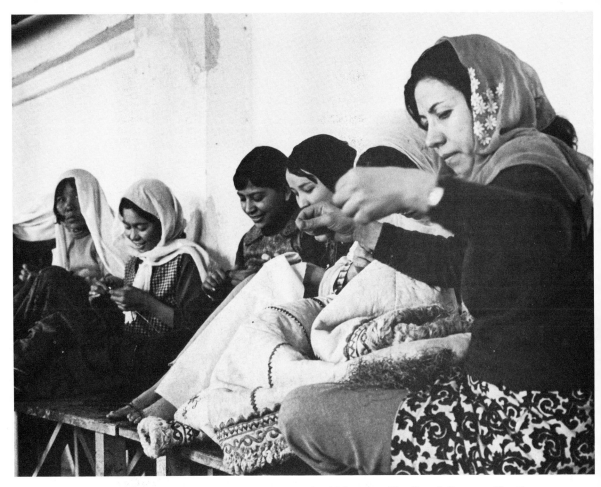

Afghan woman embroidering fur coats at the Afghanistan Handicraft Centre at Charikar, a project assisted by the United Nations Development Programme and the International Labour Organization. United Nations/K. Muldoon

The Afghans also express themselves in poetry and song. Much of the true literature of the country is unwritten, but is passed from place to place and from generation to generation in the folksongs sung by poets and wandering minstrels. These songs are very simple and direct and make up in spirited language what they may lack in polish. The main themes focus, as does Afghan poetry, on the bonds of kinship, honor, love, and war, and because their recitation is an integral part of any family celebration or festival, they form an important part of every child's education.

Folk literature is also the repository of each ethnic group's genealogies. A talented family performer learns the entire genealogy of the clan or *kheyl*, intertwining recitations with tales of the heroic exploits of important khans and historic episodes that have contributed over the decades to family pride.

Afghan music, which is monadic and modal, is more rhythmic than most oriental music, but the instruments are very similar to those of neighboring countries. Afghan orchestras usually contain several native stringed instruments, the *saranda*, *robab*, *del-roba*, *tambur*, and *santur*. The *tabla*, a small drum, is the principal percussion instrument, and the Indian harmonium (a sort of treble accordian) is often used. The tribes use more primitive instruments—the end-blown flute, a two-stringed

Men of an Afghan village celebrate a festival day by performing the national attan *dance.*
United Nations

dambura, and the heavy keg-shaped *dohol* drum—to accompany their singing and dancing.

Public dancing on holidays and festival days is a truly exciting sight. The men dance in groups of twenty to a hundred or more, revolving around a stake or a fire in ever-widening circles. They keep the center of the circle on their left in order to swing swords or guns in their right hands. The national *attan* dance begins slowly with a series of sedate figures, which gradually increase in tempo and emphasis until the final movements seem a wild frenzy. The dances are accompanied and paced by village minstrels playing the drum and reed flute, while both dancers and musicians chant the songs in chorus, punctuated by clapping, shouting, and stamping.

Recreation

Small girls in Afghanistan play house, help their mothers, and learn the domestic arts. At a very early age boys learn to use a slingshot, and will soon be driving small animals away from the fields or killing them for food. Both rural and urban children play ball games, as well as games resembling marbles and hopscotch. Team wrestling, called *ghosai*, is enjoyed all over the country, and kite fighting is popular in the towns. Many boys raise pigeons and make great sport of pigeon rustling.

Urban dwellers enjoy cards, pachisi, caroms (similar to billiards), chess, and picnics. Gambling is popular, on games and on horse racing, as well as on cock, ram, and dog fighting.

The tall, thin Afghan hound is the only dog Afghans like as pets, and both hounds and horses are bred for speed and endurance. Hunting small game is considered an excellent pastime, taking advantage of the Afghan pride in both marksmanship and horsemanship. Hunting in the country is limited to wild sheep and goats, a few bear, wolves, foxes, leopards, tigers, ibex, and plentiful game birds. Some river and lake fishing is also enjoyed.

The Afghans are extremely fond of sports such as tent pegging, which requires considerable physical strength. The national game, *buzkashi* (goat wrestling), probably is an adaptation of an ancient Central Asian sport. It is played chiefly in the north and may use ten to one hundred horsemen riding specially trained mounts. A decapitated goat is placed in a shallow ditch. On a given signal the riders dash and lean from their saddles to pick up the goat, which must be carried to a certain point and then returned and dropped in a circle at the beginning of the course. The riders work as teams, struggling to secure the goat or to keep the opposing teams from getting it, and the team of the man who finally reaches the designated circle wins. The Afghan Olympic Federation has established rules to tone down the fierceness of the game at official functions and make it safer.

Decorative Arts

Because the landscape in Afghanistan is predominantly drab expanses of sand and rock, the Afghans love decoration. They deck their horses and camels with elaborate harness, brightly colored saddlebags, artfully woven blankets. Horse-drawn carriages in the cities sport pompons, tinkling bells, and fancy fly whisks. Buses and trucks are painted with gaudy scenic panels.

Women love jewelry and invest as much as possible in gold and silver trinkets. Nomad women sew precious gold embroidery and coins on their dresses, carrying their wealth about as adornment. Cosmetic decoration is commonplace, with both sexes lining their eyes with kohl on festive occasions. Women prefer clothes of bright colors when they can afford them, with tie-dyed silks or Russian chintz in bold flowered

A description of the opening of a game of buzkashi:

The opening had a slow solemnity. Silently, step by step, the sixty horsemen surrounded the hole that held the slaughtered beast. When they stopped, it was hedged round by a tight ring. Each third of the circle bore the color of a team—the white and green of Qataghan, the brown of Meimana, the russet of Mazar-i-Sharif. For a moment this strange, enormous flower, blooming there on the ground, remained motionless.

Then all at once the lead-tipped lashes rose like a hissing nation of serpents above the fur caps, a roar of demoniac savagery, combination of all their shouts, broke over the plain, the goat's body was hidden beneath a mass of men and horses. By a transformation so sudden that no one had been able to detect the moment of its beginning, the grave and orderly band had become mere tumult, frenzy, an enormous whirlwind. Whoops, oaths,

patterns being favorites in the north. Male clothing is much more subdued, but it is not unusual to see a rugged tribesman carrying a flower or strolling along with one stuck in his rifle barrel. A wristwatch is a status symbol.

Historical Art

The country is rich in historic sites that contain architecture, sculpture, tile mosaics, and other decoration of a quality unmatched in recent centuries. These artifacts are of little interest to the average Afghan unless they are somehow connected with some glorious event in the history or genealogy of his ethnic group. In fact, unless a historic site wordless threats . . . Lashing whips ripping into muzzles and faces . . . Ebb and flow . . . Horses rearing their full height above the entangled bodies and limbs . . . Chapandaz hanging there, clinging to their horses' sides, their faces in the dust, their nails clawing, scraping the stony ground to find the headless goat, grasp it, and snatch it up. But scarcely had one succeeded than other equally fierce and powerful hands wrenched the carcass from him. It passed and passed again over the horses' withers, before their eyes, under their bellies, and fell to the ground once more. Then as though from the bottom of a foaming roller rose up a fresh surge of chests, manes, caps, and whips that swept the first away, becoming in its turn a tall wave of bodies, clothes, and blows—a wave that turned, rolling upon itself.

From *The Horsemen* by Joseph Kessel (New York: Farrar, Straus & Giroux, 1968), p. 69

is associated with a more recent mystic or locally revered saint, the rural people are apt to tear apart old tombs and temples for building materials. Enough of the art of earlier centuries has, however, been preserved to indicate the advanced level of civilization attained in these remote mountains when the important currents of earlier times were swirling through their passes and across the neighboring plains.

The very oldest artifacts—pottery, fragments of alabaster vases, copper objects, terra-cotta statuettes, awls of bone, limestone weights that now reside in the Kabul Museum—date from prehistoric times and indicate that Afghanistan was a link between the civilizations of the Tigris and Euphrates valleys and the Indus Valley as early as 3000 B.C.

It is only from the middle of the sixth century B.C., when Cyrus the

Great ruled Persia and extended his conquests to the Indus River, that written history embraces Afghanistan. Large numbers of Greek coins found throughout the country testify to Alexander's conquest of the Persians and to the Greek satrapies he left behind in the Hindu Kush after his death. Decorated glassware, sculptured ivory pieces, and bronze statuettes from this period have also been found.

When the Kushans ruled ancient Bactria in the first and second centuries A.D., they built a huge fire temple complex, reached by a monumental stone staircase extending from the plain to the summit of a large hill. Discovered in the 1950s, excavations on the site have revealed the central *cella* (inner room) where a sacred fire was tended, limestone statues and painted clay figures, and a twenty-five-line inscription in Greek characters.

The Buddhist period left behind numerous monasteries and *stupas* (shrines), decorated with large quantities of statuary and bas-reliefs, executed in shist (flaky rock) or stucco, that are collectively labeled Gandharan art. Most famous is the cliff at Bamiyan, punctuated with its two enormous effigies of Buddha and numerous caves that sheltered Buddhist monks, dating from the third to fifth centuries A.D.

In the centuries that followed, numerous impressive fortresses were built, strategically located on high cliffs above important river or caravan junctions throughout the entire Hindu Kush. The crumbling remains remind the Afghans of their ancestors' determined resistance against many invaders.

The remains of the summer palaces of the kings of Ghazni at Lash-

This coin, a silver double decadrachma, shows a Macedonian king wearing a helmet on the front, and Tyche, Goddess of fortune, on the reverse. Coins like this circulated in the Afghan region from Alexander's day on, and have frequently been found in archaeological digs. Charles Kieffer in Jeannine Auboyer, *The Art of Afghanistan,* Hamlyn House: Felham, Middlesex, England, 1968

kargah, although in ruins, testify to the magnificence of the tenth- and eleventh-century kingdom centered in southern Afghanistan. At Ghazni itself, no buildings save Mahmud's tomb have survived to remind us that its kings sponsored a university, talented teachers, learned men, and famous poets.

A few other monuments scattered about the country recall periods of earlier greatness—a single lonely minaret in the remote central mountains of Ghor Province (thirteenth-century Ghorid), the great mosque and *madrasa* at Herat (twelfth to fifteenth century), the mosque of Ali at Mazar-i-Sharif (fifteenth century).

These date from the eras when the peoples of the Hindu Kush lived on the main routes of world trade and shared the magnificence of great empires. No such impetus to artistic creation has existed in more recent centuries when the Afghans were struggling to assert their sovereignty over their homeland and to ward off the encroachments of the mighty colonial empires centered in Europe.

Gandharan sculpture from the 2nd century A.D. *This figure is a Buddhist* bodhisattva, *an enlightened being who chooses to remain on earth to assist others in their quest for salvation. Such sculpture often combines the Indian concept of how to represent the human figure with imported Greek sculptural traditions, such as heavy drapery with stiff folds and sharp ridges.* Museum of Fine Arts, Boston

Economy

Proud people and a breathtaking landscape do not conceal the fact that Afghanistan is a poor country. Only one eighth of the terrain is tillable, and precious water sources determine the location of human settlements. Economic and political development have been retarded by the rugged geography and a harsh climate as well as by ethnic and linguistic diversity. Communications links are difficult and expensive to build, making transportation costs high and slowing trade and the development of local industry.

Agriculture

Three quarters of the Afghans are subsistence farmers, meeting their own needs from their agricultural activities, perhaps selling small crop or livestock surpluses in the local market, and bartering or spending what little cash they receive on such essentials as sugar, tea, matches, and tools. Statistics published by the Afghan government in 1983 indicated that the people's average per-capita income was $167.

A third of the land that is cultivated must be irrigated, with the water coming from snowmelt from the mountains, which often causes flooding in the spring. The vagaries of the weather govern the productivity of the farmers and nomads, with never quite enough rainfall, water, or pasturage to make farming easy. Extremes of temperature between day and night and between summer and winter make harsh demands on the rural population.

Five percent of the country's land area is currently used for cultivating crops and 2 percent for orchards—the internal source of Afghan food supplies and for much of the raw material used by local industries. More land could be cultivated if irrigation were available. Cereals (wheat, corn, barley, rice) dominate the cropping pattern, occupying over 80 percent of the irrigated land and the whole of the rain-fed land. Family gardens provide vegetables for local consumption. Cotton is raised for textiles; cotton seed is the basis for oil extraction, refining, and soap industries; sugar beets are grown for sugar refining; and fruits are processed, packed, and exported. Afghanistan is also a major producer and exporter of opium and hashish, which will be difficult to change until a central government establishes nationwide political stability.

Only 3 percent of Afghanistan is forested. The trees that must have blanketed the mountains centuries ago no longer exist to retain rainfall, control flooding, and arrest erosion. Reforestation would contribute significantly to improving the environment but is almost impossible to achieve when so much of the terrain is heavily and constantly grazed by sheep and goats. Nor is reforestation an attractive activity to govern-

Afghan farmers check the condition of a field of grain at a rural development project.
United Nations

ments in developing countries, because it is a long-term process with no immediately obvious payoff.

Almost a third of Afghanistan's terrain is pasture and meadows, used for the grazing of herds of sheep and goats, which are moved by nomadic herdsmen with the seasons in search of the grass that is their principal fodder. Donkeys, horses, mules, and camels provide transportation in rural areas where roads do not exist or truck transportation is too expensive.

Forty percent of the country is either too mountainous or too dry to farm. Thus Afghanistan's limited agricultural base does not have a very large potential, yet 63 percent of the country's gross domestic income is derived from agriculture, livestock, and forestry.

Mining

Minerals are the only other natural resource that has received much attention. Natural-gas fields at Shibarghan in northern Afghanistan have been developed by the government with Soviet assistance, with the

Herdsmen in a nomad camp.   United Nations/H. K. Lall

output used either to run local factories or exported to the U.S.S.R. The announcement in the 1986–91 Five Year Plan that natural-gas production would increase 260 percent may indicate discovery of an important new gas field.

Business Week reported in 1980 that Soviet surveys had found significant quantities of oil, copper, barite, bauxite, beryl, iron ore, fluorspar, coal, chrome, and possibly uranium, but political instability and internal fighting have prevented development of these resources. No estimates of the extent of these resources are available, nor is any exploration and development of mineral resources by countries other than the U.S.S.R. permitted.

Handicrafts

Cottage crafts have traditionally played an important role in the Afghan economy, employing more people than modern industry and mining.

Nomadic herdsmen bring their flock of sheep to their camp.   United Nations/H. K. Lall

A nomadic herdsman waits his turn to get his goats vaccinated at the animal health clinic in Kandahar. United Nations/H. K. Lall

Hand-woven carpets, karakul pelts, and lapis lazuli jewelry are in demand in foreign markets. The Afghans themselves make extensive use of crafts in the local economy.

Industry

The industrial and commercial sector of the Afghan economy employs only a quarter of the country's workers, and accounts for about a third of the gross domestic product. Industry, mines, and energy bring in a fifth of the country's income, with the largest industrial enterprises owned by the state. Trade accounts for a little over 7 percent, construction almost 5 percent, and transportation and communications 3 percent. The professional and services functions that are becoming

Herdsmen in the Kunar valley move their goats to another grazing ground. United Nations/Photo by Ray Witlin

dominant in Western economies barely exist in Afghanistan.

Industry in Afghanistan is pretty much confined to the processing of raw materials: cotton ginning and textile weaving, edible-oil extraction, and sugar refining. State-owned industrial enterprises produce cement, sugar, textiles, and metal products.

Afghanistan is richly endowed with potential sources of hydro power in its lofty snow-clad mountains. An increasing number of hydroelectric plants have been established, generally near the major cities, where demand for electric power is large.

External Trade

Traditionally Afghanistan's trade has been dominated by exports of agricultural and animal products in exchange for manufactured goods and foods. Today export of natural gas (at well below world market prices) to the Soviet Union is in first place, followed by fresh and dried fruit, and carpets and rugs. The export of karakul skins has dropped over the years as fashion demand for lambskin has declined. Major imports continue to include machinery, petroleum products, textiles, sugar, edible oils, tea, and yarn.

The Soviet Union is by far the principal trading partner, handling 65 percent of Afghanistan's total trade, with Afghan raw materials exchanged for machinery, equipment, and other essential commodities imported from the Soviet Union. Trade with West Germany, Japan, the United Kingdom, and Hong Kong usually accounts for about 20 percent, with the rest of Afghanistan's exports going to Pakistan and India.

Physical Infrastructure

Afghanistan's limited infrastructure (a term development experts use to include public works like transportation networks, utility systems, and water supplies) is a major constraint on the country's development. A loop-road network connects the major cities and border points, but mountain and desert villages are often inaccessible during winter and spring weather. Civil aviation (Bakhtar Afghan Airways) connects the major cities and towns, and the Soviets have built extensive military aviation facilities. Only the major cities have electric power, with 90 percent of this power coming from hydro sources. Piped water supplies are also confined to urban areas. Few villages have adequate water delivery or sewage-disposal systems.

Development Efforts

The Afghan government, recognizing the need to encourage economic and social change, started long-range planning in 1954. Four successive Five Year Plans were adopted under the monarchy. The governments that followed the coups in 1973 and 1979 allocated even more resources to the effort to eliminate backwardness, increase the national product, bring about progressive social changes, and raise the living standards of the people.

Governments involved in centralized economic planning must have staff working in that area. Under the communists an agency called the State Planning Committee (S.P.C.) is responsible for preparing an annual plan as well as midterm plans for various sectors, guided by the basic objectives listed above. The S.P.C. also coordinates sectoral planning activities and monitors plan implementation.

While the government gives highest priority to the development of agriculture, the guerrilla war limited the implementation of most devel-

Afghan villagers display a hide for sale.   United Nations

An irrigation dam under construction in Kunar Province. United Nations/Photo by Ray Witlin

opment projects to the Kabul area, as well as draining off a third of the Afghan budget to support the military. Nonmilitary allocations in the 1980s directed 10 percent of the budget to agriculture, 15 percent to industry, 16 percent to mining, 6 percent to energy, 24 percent to transportation and communications (mostly construction), 25 percent to the social sector (education, public health, water supplies, and so on) and 4 percent to other expenses.

Financing of development programs and projects is constrained by shortages of both internal and external resources. Trained and skilled managers and workers are in short supply, as are administrators and teachers. The government relies on Soviets to fill the gap. It will be difficult to expand the present tax base and to draw greater revenues from public enterprises. Receipt of external assistance from Western governments ceased with the Saur Revolution, and aid from international organizations such as the World Bank and Asian Development

Farmers open an irrigation canal to water their fields. United Nations/Photo by Ray Witlin

Bank dropped sharply after 1979 as war spread across the country.

The U.S.S.R. has become the principal source of financial support to Afghanistan. Between 1966 and 1976 Soviet aid totaled $750 million, while American assistance in the same decade dropped to $150 million. From December 1976 to the December 1979 invasion, Soviet military and economic aid came to roughly $1 billion, targeted at major extensions of hydroelectric and irrigation schemes, a rail and road bridge across the Amu Darya River at Termez, development of fertilizer production, and expansion of natural-gas production. Economic assistance provided between 1979 and 1986 exceeded $1.6 billion, while military assistance is believed to have exceeded $5 billion. In 1985 (the last year for which a figure is available) Moscow pledged $320 million in new economic aid—the second largest commitment since 1979. A third of this aid was slated for food and consumer goods grants, while the rest was directed to hydroelectric power expansion, road construction and modernization, and technical schools.

Soviet aid is in the form of long-term, low-interest loans, with the salaries of more than 9,000 Soviet advisers and technicians paid by the Afghan government. The amounts of assistance provided far exceed Afghanistan's economic capacity to repay; instead, the U.S.S.R. expects political repayment in the form of loyal support of the communist bloc.

Development Bottlenecks

Very little of the development assistance provided to Afghanistan in the 1960s and 1970s trickled down to the rural farmers. Most of its benefits

Afghan workers break rocks for road construction.   United Nations/Photo by Ray Witlin

An Afghan in Paktia Province surveys the remains of his home after a Soviet air strike.
Christopher Brown

were enjoyed by the urban elite. The left-wing radicals who seized control of the government in 1978 tried to correct the inequities, but the reforms that the Kabul government instituted in rural areas have generally alienated more people than they have helped, largely by ignoring the deeply ingrained social patterns that structure rural life. Before the Soviet invasion, the communist government began a land-reform program without having any clear idea how much tillable land was in the hands of absentee landlords. (Actually, about half of the agricultural land is owned by the cultivators.) Simply giving land to the farmer, however, does not solve his problems, because he must have funds to buy seed and other necessities and access to irrigation water. The government failed to provide credit to the farmers, forcing them to borrow from local lenders, who soon gained the same kind of control formerly held by the landlords. The rural farmers were also very suspicious that government land-distribution schemes were an attempt to replace the autonomy of local leaders with central control.

After a few months, many of the P.D.P.A. government's agrarian measures, which had been introduced with much fanfare, were quietly dropped. The attempt at land reform, combined with guerrilla warfare and other "reforms," so disrupted Afghan agriculture that a previously

Too old and too young to fight, a grandfather and grandson pass the time in a refugee camp in Pakistan, waiting until they can return to their village across the border. United Nations/John Isaac

self-sufficient country was faced with a large deficit of grain that the Soviets had to make up.

Other government decrees that were intended to modernize Afghanistan by ending archaic practices—canceling peasant debts, forbidding the charging of interest on loans, outlawing the bride price and arranged marriages, expanding coeducation, discouraging strictures of religion— were brutally implemented, clashing headlong with ancient customs and arousing violent antagonism among the very people they were supposed to help.

The war devastated the rural economy, particularly in the provinces bordering Pakistan. There brutal scorched-earth tactics adopted by the Soviets to interdict resistance supplies across the border reduced hostile villages and towns to piles of mud and brick rubble. Irrigation systems were deliberately destroyed, crops burned, livestock killed, and water sources contaminated in an effort to starve out farmers who supported the rebels. This destruction of housing, food, and water supplies was followed by aerial surveillance intended to make it impossible for the Afghan families to return to their homes. Instead, the able-bodied men worked in the fields and vineyards by day when they could, and fought by night.

Today there are shortages of such basic foods as wheat in the 50-mile (80-kilometer) belt along the Pakistan frontier. In other areas periodic scarcities of vegetables, oils, rice, sugar, and tea are caused by damage to the transportation system. The supply of local meat seems adequate. The Soviets had to import food not only to feed their own troops but also to sustain civilian populations in the cities—which increased steadily because of the influx of rural refugees. The once-prosperous cotton crop dropped in size, and in Kabul firewood and charcoal were rationed. Industry suffered from shortages of labor, raw materials, and fuel.

World Power Politics

In February 1988 the regular evening television schedule in the Soviet Union was interrupted to transmit an announcement by Chairman Mikhail Gorbachev that Soviet troops would withdraw from Afghanistan after the completion of United Nations negotiations in Geneva. This decision indicated that the Politburo had measured the cost of the Afghan venture, concluded that there was no chance of victory there, and decided that the risks of withdrawal must be taken.

The implications of this decision are enormous. Soviet officials now insist that the P.D.P.A. failed to make Afghanistan into a truly communist state, so they have no obligation to maintain it under the Brezhnev Doctrine (which held that once a country became communist, it must remain communist, and the U.S.S.R. had the right to intervene to make sure it did). The Soviet troops sent by Chairman Brezhnev in the 1970s into weak Third World countries like Afghanistan, Angola, and Ethiopia produced little return and caused a great deal of trouble for the Soviet Union. Now the Kremlin leaders seek to revise their relations with the outside world.

U.N. Negotiations

In addition to annual resolutions by the U.N. General Assembly condemning the Soviet invasion, negotiations were carried on for several years by the Undersecretary General of the United Nations, Diego Cordovez, between the Kabul government and the government of Pakistan in an effort to end the fighting. The Afghan resistance leaders were not included in these talks, nor did the Pakistan government talk directly to the Afghans, whose communist government in Kabul it did not recognize. The Undersecretary carried messages between the delegations, and the Pakistanis tried to line up the support of the resistance leaders headquartered in Peshawar for any agreement reached.

The different parties involved in the U.N. negotiations wanted different ingredients included in the withdrawal plan. The Soviets have some 300 economic agreements with the P.D.P.A. government, and hope these will be honored in the future. They also planned to leave behind some 9,000 Soviet advisers (including military advisers) when their troops departed. Knowing Afghan enthusiasm for revenge and lack of enthusiasm for strong government, it is hard to see how resistance leaders, who have fought bitterly for eight years and lost family members and homes, would permit foreigners to go on directing the affairs

Reconstruction of villages and vital water systems will be necessary when Afghan refugees return to their homes.   United Nations

of their country. In fact, it is hard to imagine that Soviet advisers would be safe after the Soviet Army removed its protection.

Although the Soviets no longer insisted on this as a condition for withdrawal, Pakistan wanted to put in place in Kabul an interim government that included the Afghan resistance leaders headquartered in Peshawar; this would permit the *mujahidin* to stop fighting and the refugees to return home. Pakistani leaders believed this could not happen if General Najibullah's government remained in place in Kabul. They urged the Peshawar resistance leaders (over whom they had some influence) to agree to participate in a coalition before the Soviet Army left, which would legitimize the Afghan government and preempt the resistance leaders inside Afghanistan. No such agreement was reached, although arms and drug trafficking may so destablize the frontier provinces on both sides of the border that Pakistan's internal stability could be threatened. The new civilian prime minister, Benazir Bhotto, has reaffirmed her country's support for the Afghan resistance.

The P.D.P.A. government, on the other hand, wanted, but did not obtain, a total cease-fire during the withdrawal period in the hope it could avoid being overthrown. Its leaders feared a bloodbath otherwise.

The crucial factor in the accords was the Soviet withdrawal plan. The United States and Pakistan wanted a schedule for a rapid withdrawal, with Soviet combat forces being the first to leave. The United States also pressed for an end to Soviet military aid and the withdrawal of military advisers. The Soviets finally agreed to a nine-month withdrawal schedule, contingent on the termination of arms shipments to the *mujahidin* from outside sources. The Soviets made no promises, however, to terminate their own military assistance to the Kabul government, and a tacit understanding was apparently reached before the accords were signed in April that aid to the resistance would continue in symmetrical proportion to Soviet aid.

The withdrawal began in May, and the goal of having all the Soviet troops across the border by mid-February 1989 was met. Resistance forces immediately took over many rural outposts, while the Soviets concentrated on providing support to the Afghan army in holding the provincial capitals. Soviet air strikes were flown across the northern border to maintain control of important towns in Afghan Turkistan against resistance attacks. The Soviet ambassador also attempted unsuccessfully to negotiate a coalition government with *mujahidin* participation.

The *mujahid* leaders made it clear that they had no intention of laying down their arms until a government acceptable to them took charge in Kabul. Even if the flow of outside arms across the Pakistan border was halted, the resistance had stockpiled enough arms to support many more months of fighting.

Everyone concerned wanted an acceptable system for verifying the withdrawal. The United States and the Soviet Union both agreed to assume responsibility for monitoring an orderly withdrawal, and the United Nations Security Council approved a fifty-man U.N. observer team to assist them. The United Nations Undersecretary General offered to mediate among the Afghan factions after the accords were signed, and Prince Sadruddin Aga Khan was appointed United Nations relief coordinator for Afghanistan to supervise refugee repatriation and coordinate international development assistance.

Soviet Interests in Afghanistan

Experts on Afghanistan and the Soviet Union will probably debate for years to come whether the Soviet invasion of Afghanistan was a short-term response to a crisis within Afghanistan or part of a long-term Kremlin strategy to reach warm-water ports on the Indian Ocean.

Russia has pushed hungrily against her southern neighbors ever since the reign of the czars, and many observers pointed to the advantage gained by the Soviet Union in threatening the oil resources of the Persian Gulf, thereby destabilizing the free world.

Whatever the global intentions of the U.S.S.R. were, the immediate concern of the Kremlin leaders in 1979 was to protect a huge investment, both in money and prestige, that the Soviet Union had made in Afghanistan after 1950. The country was disintegrating into anarchy, and unless drastic action was taken, a government whose leaders professed to be socialists was about to slip out of the communist orbit by default. This represented a failure in Soviet foreign policy that only a military action could prevent.

Internal Effects of the Change in Soviet Policy

The price Moscow paid for its occupation of Afghanistan was much higher than expected because the Afghan resistance was so fierce and effective. The Soviets overlooked the fact that the Afghans are tough and independent, and love to fight. Nine years of resistance kept some 115,000 crack Soviet troops at bay, and proved clearly how difficult Afghanistan is to govern. The long military occupation was very expensive: Supplies had to be shipped in both for Soviet soldiers and to provide food and fuel for the Afghan cities. Moscow admits that 35,000 Soviet casualties resulted from the fighting, with 15,000 killed. Soldiers returning from Afghan service were bitter that their sacrifices were not recognized. Many of them had drug and readjustment problems. Parents of slain soldiers questioned the worth of their losses.

Some 80,000 Afghan guerillas and a million Afghan civilians are believed to have died, and a third of the population fled the country. This carnage and disruption caused widespread apprehension about Soviet intentions, not only among the Afghans but also in other Third World countries, particularly those that are also Moslem.

Less easy to assess will be the impact of the humiliation of withdrawal on the Soviet Army, a humiliation that was emphasized when their troops were harassed as they departed. Like the United States after Vietnam, the U.S.S.R. will survive its humiliation, but the impact on national attitudes may shape the country's future.

Another real concern will be the effect that the successful Moslem stand in Afghanistan may have on the 24 million Moslem citizens in the Central Asian Republics of the U.S.S.R. Next door in Iran the triumphant Ayatollah Khomeini and his supporters have spread the propaganda of Islamic nationalism among the Shiahs. If Moslem fundamentalists gain control in Afghanistan, will their example inspire revolutionary tendencies within the Soviet Union? The Kremlin may intend to provide continuing air support to the Afghan army from across the northern border, directed by Soviet advisers within the country, to prevent this from happening. All provincial capitals are within bomber range of airbases north of the Amu Darya, and such a policy could be justified as "military assistance."

The world has largely forgotten the fact that the Emirate of Bokhara and the Khanate of Khiva, Moslem states north of the Afghan border, were forcibly taken over and suppressed by the Red Army in 1920, and that their rulers took refuge in Afghanistan. The Afghan king, Amanullah, sent aid to the Moslem rebels in Central Asia who continued to fight against Soviet domination and who used Afghanistan as a haven for resting, regrouping, and obtaining weapons as they carried on their struggle—an earlier version of what has gone on across the Afghan-Pakistan border in the 1980s. (Interestingly enough, the Soviet press used the same term for the Afghan resistance that it did for the Central Asian resistance in the 1920s: *basmachi*, meaning "bandits.") When they were finally defeated, hundreds of thousands of Tajiks, Uzbeks, Turkmen, and Kirghiz from Central Asia settled permanently in northern Afghanistan, where they and their children remained to take up arms again against the Soviet invaders.

The Soviets mistakenly assumed that these ethnic groups would welcome their Soviet kin in the communization of Afghanistan. After Taraki seized power in 1978, many Soviet Central Asians were sent to Afghanistan as interpreters, technicians, bureaucrats, and teachers. During the initial invasion in 1979 large numbers of the troops used were Central Asians. The policy backfired when the Central Asians sympathized with the Moslem rebels and were reluctant to fight them. The Soviet Central Asians were quickly withdrawn and replaced by Slavs from northern Russia, but ethnic consciousness may have been raised within the Soviet Union by this miscalculation. One very large question following the Soviet withdrawal from Afghanistan will be the psychological effect of returning Soviet advisers on the Central Asian population, which is still unhappy with Russian rule. Protests, strikes, and ethnic unrest have been occurring in a number of the Soviet Republics since 1987 and must worry the Soviet leadership.

External Effects of the New Soviet Policy

The new policy toward Afghanistan resulted from the change in leadership within the Soviet Union, which brought with it a major revision in attitudes toward Soviet economic and social problems. The Afghan invasion occurred under Chairman Brezhnev, in a decade when relations were strained between the United States and the Soviet Union. Power vacuums presented opportunities for meddling in Third World countries, which the Soviet Union exploited with considerable tactical skill. The fall of the shah and taking of American hostages in Iran paralyzed Washington to the point that Afghanistan must have looked like easy prey to the Kremlin.

In 1985 leadership in Moscow changed. The new chairman, Mikhail Gorbachev, recognized that the Soviet economy must be modernized if the U.S.S.R. is to remain a leading world power. The years of military effort in Afghanistan produced only a stalemate, and the enormous political and social cost of the Afghan war became a liability that the Politburo decided it must shed. New strategies were needed to remove this burden.

The Intermediate-range Nuclear Force treaty between the United States and the Soviet Union in 1987 provided the first major step. If the two superpowers can reach further arms-control agreements, reducing the tensions between them, the dangers posed by the forms of government adopted by weak countries on or near their borders should diminish. A return to peace in Afghanistan could be the first step in defining new superpower relationships with Third World countries in an increasingly interdependent world.

United States Interests in Afghanistan

The Kremlin maintained during the Soviet occupation of Afghanistan that the United States was the principal imperialist power instigating the rebellion. American policy toward Afghanistan since the Second World War contradicts this claim. Although the United States made loans and grants and provided technical assistance to Afghanistan from the 1950s onward, there was no attempt to establish dominant American influence. Successive administrations in Washington indicated that they understood that Afghanistan's location made it necessary for Kabul to maintain good relations with the Soviet Union. In fact, U.S. policy made it quite clear that Afghanistan was not considered an important country. It had few natural resources and relatively little strategic importance. U.S. policy remained remarkably consistent, under both King Zahir and President Daud: The United States attempted to maintain a presence in the country by providing assistance in economic development, and encouraged the Afghans to cherish their independence.

Despite all the indications that the Taraki regime installed after the Saur Revolution was communist and aligned with the Soviet Union, Washington did not protest the forcible seizure of power in Kabul by a minority or accuse the Soviet Union of being behind the coup. American economic, cultural, educational, and Peace Corps programs were continued. Some American officials argued that aid should be stopped, and that the failure of the United States to react more forcefully to the 1978 coup led the Soviets to believe that Washington would take little action when they invaded in 1979. Those who argued the opposite— that the United States could hardly compete with the U.S.S.R. for influence in a backward country lying along the Soviet border and governed by communists who controlled a Soviet-equipped army— prevailed.

A drastic reassessment of the importance of that whole area of the world was forced on the United States in January 1979, when the shah fled from Iran and an interim Islamic government was established there. Washington's maintenance of cordial relations with the Kabul regime lasted until February 1979, when the American Ambassador, Adolph Dubs, was kidnapped by unidentified persons who held him hostage for the release of imprisoned opponents of the regime. The Afghan police, under the direction of Soviet officials, stormed the hotel room where Dubs was being held, resulting in his death. Even then American aid was continued on a smaller scale, although the Peace Corps was withdrawn and the size of the American Embassy staff reduced.

In November 1979 Iranian revolutionaries stormed the American Embassy in Tehran, seizing hostages whom they vowed to hold until the deposed shah was returned to Iran. In that same month a Pakistani mob—inflamed by rumors that the CIA was responsible for the seizure by terrorists a few weeks earlier of the Great Mosque in Mecca—burned the American Embassy in Islamabad. Top American officials were completely engrossed with these problems when, less than six weeks later, the Soviet Army invaded Afghanistan. Was the timing coincidental? The Soviet takeover in Kabul, following soon after the triumph of the Ayatollah Khomeini in Iran, completely changed the strategic situation in the Persian Gulf area, on which much of the free world depends for oil resources. Only after those crises did American President Jimmy Carter publicly announce to the Soviet Union that the United States would defend its interests in the Gulf.

American aid programs were ended with the Soviet invasion, and our relations with the Afghan government limited to a small diplomatic mission in Kabul, which maintained contact with the Ministry of Foreign Affairs' Office of Protocol on necessary administrative and consular matters. (The embassy was closed as the last Soviet troops left.)

The United States did send assistance to the Afghan *mujahidin*, however, both because Americans admired the bravery of the Afghans and wanted them to maintain their independence and because it served our own interests. When the Soviets were busy fighting in Afghanistan, they had fewer resources to cause trouble elsewhere. Afghanistan could not be used as a staging area for Soviet moves toward the Persian Gulf as long as three quarters of the country was in the hands of guerrillas.

In the earlier years of the war, American assistance financed the transfer to the *mujahidin* of old Soviet weapons from stocks in Egypt and elsewhere. More recently the United States provided between $300 million to $650 million in aid annually, including Stinger missiles and other equipment designed to shoot down the helicopter gunships and jetfighters that were so devastating resistance villages. This kind of support was far too limited to permit the *mujahidin* to drive out the Soviet Army, but it confined the enemy to the main cities, towns, and isolated military posts, prevented the military from taking control of the countryside, and brought the conflict to a stalemate.

Afghanistan's Future International Role

Afghanistan was, after 1879, a buffer state, separating the empires of Russia and Great Britain. When Britain withdrew from the Indian subcontinent in 1947, it left behind the independent states of India and Pakistan. The dominant world powers were the United States and the Soviet Union, which have since World War II competed for influence in the new countries of the Third World. Their rivalries led the United States to enter into a security alliance with Pakistan, and the Soviet Union to provide massive economic and military assistance to India, while both powers courted Afghanistan.

In the quarter century following 1947, the Afghan leadership successfully played the superpowers against each other, taking assistance from both while maintaining Afghanistan's neutrality. Because the United States could not provide military assistance while Afghanistan was quarreling with Pakistan about Pushtun self-determination, Afghan military modernization was financed by the Soviet Union. The 1978 Saur Revolution was a military action, and the political leaders who seized control at that time looked to the U.S.S.R. as their model.

If Soviet military support is completely withdrawn, control of the central government in Kabul must inevitably change because the Afghan communist party commands so little support. In a country where blood revenge is a fundamental concept of honor, the P.D.P.A. piled up an enormous debt to be avenged. The Soviet Union may, however, go on providing massive military support to the Afghan army, even after the troops are withdrawn, hoping thereby to sustain the communist regime in Kabul and maintain control of the provincial capitals.

The shape of the country's future and its role in world affairs depend very much on which of the many competing Afghan factions wins control.

Reconciliation

The heroism of the *mujahidin* in standing up to the Soviet Army tends to obscure the fact that the struggle in Afghanistan is not only a conflict between guerrilla fighters and foreign invaders, but also a conflict between conservative religious forces that cling to traditional ways and modernizing trends that bring new outlooks and new values. This conflict is not new in Afghanistan. King Amanullah lost his throne when he moved too quickly to revise education and change the role of women. Zahir Shah failed in his effort to turn his government into a constitutional monarchy. Muhammad Daud made Afghanistan a republic, but without any mechanisms for orderly political succession.

The Saur Revolution completely disrupted orderly progress in economic and social development when diverse groups of Afghans opposed the communist political philosophy of the P.D.P.A. government. Afghan patriots turned to guerrilla warfare when the Soviet Army came to the rescue of that government. There were many players in this game, with a wide variety of motivations. And because the Afghans themselves are not in agreement about what kind of future they aspire to, the country could suffer chaos for years to come.

Divisions Within Afghanistan

The withdrawal of the Soviet Army will not solve Afghanistan's problems. Some foreign observers have estimated that there may be as many as 300 different resistance groups, with between 800 and 1,200 commanders, each intent on his own particular agenda. Some groups are run by political or religious factions, but the great majority follow local leaders who have flexible ties with neighboring groups or with the organized opposition parties headquartered in Peshawar. Ethnic or tribal composition tends to determine the makeup of each local front, and in spite of almost a decade of waging guerrilla warfare, the many groups have failed to get together and form any kind of united opposition government.

Only occasionally do these groups cooperate with each other. For example, there are seven resistance groups with headquarters across the border in Peshawar. Most of the leaders are Pushtuns, but at least one is Tajik. In 1985 these groups formed a resistance alliance called the "Islamic Unity of Afghan Mujahidin." This coalition represented two widely differing points of view, which may be characterized as "Moslem fundamentalist" (made up of groups that have actively opposed the Kabul government since the end of the monarchy in 1973) and "moderate nationalist" (groups that in fact represent regional interests and have agreed to form a common front, and whose leaders had ties to the

Young dancers ready to perform at a Jeshan *(Independence Day)* Festival *in Kabul. Will their generation be able to live in a truly independent nation?*   United Nations

former monarchy). Although all the groups professed to have political platforms, they were each dominated by the personalities of their leaders.

The two factions agreed that their goal is a nonaligned Afghanistan, open to both East and West, but were in conflict as to whether a new Afghanistan should be an Islamic theocracy, a constitutional monarchy, an Islamic republic, or a secular democratic republic. These groups gained most of the media's attention because their headquarters in Peshawar were accessible to Western journalists, and they served as the conduit for the flow of foreign arms and humanitarian assistance coming from the outside world to Afghanistan.

On the other hand, the Peshawar leaders alienated many Afghans with their constant bickering, corruption, bureaucratic opportunism, failure to develop coherent strategy and work together, and the fact that most of their leaders were operating individually as politicians outside the country rather than leading the internal struggle inside the country. The Peshawar leaders did conclude agreements with the internal commanders, who traded their political support for funds, weapons, ammunition, medical supplies and assistance, and other aid.

In 1986 several of the alliance leaders visited Washington, the UN, Europe, the Islamic Conference meeting in Morocco, and Saudi Arabia in search of recognition and additional assistance. Leaders of two of the alliance groups in Peshawar refused to join the mission and publicized the fissures that kept the coalition from being a representative opposition movement. The alliance leadership rotated successfully among the various leaders, and committees worked to set up education and social services and the coordination of outside assistance. But because the leaders never agreed on tactics and the course Afghanistan should follow in the future, the alliance was never an effective government in exile. The ideological conflict between the religious fundamentalists and the nationalists will persist, as will the conflict between tradition and modernization, causing continuing strife in the future.

Within Afghanistan the position of other resistance leaders was less certain. Strong Pushtun leaders in Peshawar might agree to halt enough of the Pushtun resistance for a Pushtun coalition to successfully govern the Pushtun areas south of the Hindu Kush, permitting a withdrawal of Soviet troops from that area. The other ethnic groups may be less willing to lay down their arms and permit themselves again to be governed by Pushtuns, particularly by the conservative Pushtuns who led the fundamentalist resistance groups in Peshawar. Pushtun arrogance and domination have been resented in the past, and other ethnic groups have fought communist control just as fiercely in their own areas as the Pushtuns have fought, receiving only limited outside support through Pakistan. These other ethnic groups will not be eager to relinquish control over their own affairs to conservative Pushtuns who are not apt to support real reform and fair political representation. Too many young Afghans have proved their mettle in the long years of guerrilla warfare, and have assumed leadership roles and responsibility that in the past belonged to older men. These new leaders expect to have their say in any future Afghan government.

The non-Pushtun resistance groups seem to have two very different outlooks. North of the Hindu Kush, the Tajiks and the Turkish communities were largely motivated by a sheer determination to hold on to their land and flocks and run their own affairs. Their resistance to the Soviets was intensified by memories, among many of the refugee families, of the loss of homes in Central Asia to the Red Army a half century ago. They harassed departing Soviet troops and will actively resist Soviet plans to continue exploiting the natural-gas fields and other Afghan natural resources located north of the Hindu Kush.

A very different outlook exists in the rugged central provinces of Afghanistan, where the Hazarahs isolated themselves in their mountain fastnesses. A coalition of pro-Iranian groups ran affairs there and was the major recipient of Iranian support, and the area served as a refuge for the resistance. The Hazarahs, sharing the Shiah faith of Iran, never liked the second-class status to which the Sunni Pushtuns relegated them and were hopeful that their future status would include autonomy from Kabul. Since their area is largely inaccessible and has little to offer in the way of exploitable resources, the Kabul government may ignore the Hazarahs and leave them to their own devices.

Afghan Motivations

It is also important to remember that the individual *mujahid* in Afghanistan did not fight for some lofty national goal or patriotic ideal. He fought, as Afghans have fought for centuries, to defend his family and individual village or valley, the birthright that he believed in—buoyed by a deep religious faith that God gave him this birthright, expects him to fight for it, and will reward him in the hereafter for defending it. Fighting for a larger cause is outside his usual way of thinking unless a dynamic leader inspires him and leads the way, as Ismail Khan was able to do in Herat, and Ahmad Shah Massoud in the northeast.

Beyond his birthright, there have been a variety of other motivations for resisting the Kabul government, which have varied from ethnic group to ethnic group as well as from class to class. The rural people have never known a well-organized central government or much efficiency in public administration, nor do they want a powerful government interfering in their affairs. The country has always been a loose alliance of diverse groups, whose chiefs have given limited allegiance to the rulers in Kabul but have been accustomed to maintaining local control over local affairs. The king was always regarded as the first among equals, and his authority rested on the loyalty he cultivated among the tribes by granting privileges, subsidies, political power, and economic benefits to their leaders.

The communist leaders who seized control in 1978 were commoners who had never participated in this symbiotic arrangement and failed to duplicate it. Their attempts to impose central authority by force immediately alienated the bulk of the population, which considered local autonomy their prerogative. The P.D.P.A. leaders also tried to counter the influence of Islam, which they considered reactionary, further alienating rural populations whose religious conservativism is deeply ingrained. Clumsy attempts at land reform without arranging alternate sources of credit and irrigation water for the farmers alienated both the farmers and the powerful rural elite.

The way in which the revolution took place also offended the strong sense of honor of the dominant Pushtuns. The kings of Afghanistan had been Pushtun for two hundred years, and although President Daud replaced the monarchy with a republic, he was still a member of the royal family and acceptable to the Pushtun tribes. When the communists killed Daud and members of his family in 1978, they destroyed one of the few symbols of unity that held Afghanistan together. In the Pushtun code of honor, this unjustified slaughter of respected leaders called for revenge.

The brutality and terrorism with which the P.D.P.A. set about eliminating its opponents and enforcing its new policies fueled urban resistance. Not only were the educated Afghans who did not support the P.D.P.A. deprived of any say in national affairs, but also their very lives were threatened. Opposition to the communists became to them not only a struggle for civil liberties, but also a fight for individual survival, causing many of those not arrested to flee the country.

The final indignity was, of course, the arrival of Soviet troops on Afghan soil, transforming an internal civil conflict into war against a foreign invader. Afghan history is a litany of foreign invasions, against which the Afghans have never failed to struggle with a fierce and fanatic determination. Afghan tribesmen have always been armed, have taken great pride in their military prowess, and had rebelled long before foreign powers began to supply additional weapons. A handicraft arms industry has existed in the Sulayman Mountains of Pakistan for decades, producing exact copies of every kind of hand weapon imaginable, and every Pushtun tribesman acquires weapons at an early age, carries them constantly, and takes great pride in his reputation as a fighter and a marksman.

Training camps for the *mujahidin* to learn to use more modern weapons and more efficient guerrilla tactics were established in the rugged mountains along the Pakistan border—by the many Pushtun resistance groups who were welcomed by their cousins across the border and who depended on Pakistan as their source of supply and a haven for their families when their villages were destroyed. The other major arms suppliers—China, Egypt, Saudi Arabia, the Gulf states—funneled their shipments through Iran and Pakistan, although the resistance leaders complained that they received only part of those sent through Pakistan and generally paid high prices for what they did acquire. They accused the Pakistan Army of skimming off the sophisticated anti-aircraft weapons and missiles, and suggested that the Pakistanis regarded this as some compensation for their burden of caring for over three million Afghan refugees in camps along the border. Pakistan also had to contend with Soviet military strikes against its territory as well as frequent terrorist incidents that occurred when resistance movements in the border area became too effective.

The resistance support provided through Pakistan was not all the Kabul government had to contend with, however. It had no more control over most other areas of Afghanistan than it did over the provinces on the Pakistan border. Effective resistance was mounted in many areas of the interior that received little or no help from outside the country. In the central mountains, for example, the Hazarah people completely severed their ties with Kabul. Because the terrain is rugged, with very limited access by road, the guerrillas there quite effectively prevented any penetration by Afghan or Soviet Army units. Much of their military equipment came from Afghan Army deserters, who brought it with them. An independent administration was set up to run hospitals and schools, collect taxes and settle disputes, and the Hazarahs (who are mostly Shiah Moslems) looked to fundamentalist Iran as their inspiration in seeking independence from the Pushtun-dominated Kabul government.

Reconciliation After the Soviet Withdrawal

Having achieved their primary objective of getting rid of foreign troops, the resistance must now find ways of reuniting and reconstructing a badly fragmented country. The most difficult problem of all will be to form a government in Kabul that commands the allegiance of the many ethnic, religious, military, and political groups. The resistance groups have only begun to espouse truly national principles, and regional institutions have started to function in several areas—the first sign of unified purposes. Councils made up of both traditional political and military leaders actually coordinate public services—food supplies, health care, schools, shelter, and other support—in the Kandahar area and in the northeastern provinces of Afghanistan. Now the task of expanding such transprovincial and multiparty organizations is essential to the development of a national political entity that can replace the present communist government.

The UN negotiators recommended a neutral government. The problem is to forge an acceptable coalition, one that all the major groups will accept. The Soviets have held talks with the exiled Zahir Shah on the subject, but neither he nor any other Afghan leader now on the stage commands the respect needed to paper over the differences among the many resistance groups.

The Need for Leadership

The most positive thing that could occur in Afghanistan would be for a strong Afghan leader to emerge who could reunite his people and rally them in support of the national cause. This kind of leader has been the country's salvation in the past, although Afghans of that stature seem to appear only about once a century. Without such a leader, Afghanistan could continue in a state of chaos, with the many competing groups intriguing with each other and jockeying for power. Without the cohesion of a strong leader, the government could well disintegrate into anarchy.

Without a central government that commands national respect and obedience, there can also be much further bloodshed. The Soviets, needless to say, wanted to leave in an orderly way, without guerrilla harassment as they went. They intend to continue their assistance to the Afghan army and to leave their advisers behind. Without a central authority that can bring an end to the fighting, however, Afghans bent on revenge could attempt to slaughter both Soviet advisers and the Afghan politicians and military forces connected with the P.D.P.A. government. This possibility presents a nightmare for those appointed to monitor and verify an orderly transition.

Reconstruction

Aside from the task of maintaining order, any future Afghan government must also cope with the gargantuan task of reconstructing the country. The return to normal life will be slow and costly.

Five million refugees want to return to their homes, but international relief organizations say that over half of Afghanistan's 24,000 villages have been partially or wholly devastated by the war, displacing one third to one half of the rural population. Many of the refugee women and children will find their husbands and fathers dead or wounded. The homes to which they return will be in ruins, the fields untended, the orchards splintered, the irrigation ditches crushed, the livestock gone. Only half of the land that could be farmed before the Soviet invasion is now usable, and the yield on the remaining land has dropped a quarter. A rural population that was poor before the troubles will face even greater poverty as it struggles with the psychological trauma of readjustment.

Need for Outside Assistance

Large sums of money will be needed from outside donors for resettlement and rehabilitation: Rural areas will require health clinics, schools, new animals, seeds and fertilizer, repairs to destroyed irrigation systems, agricultural cooperatives, marketing arrangements, credit. Relief agencies estimate that two or three years will be needed just to rebuild the infrastructure to produce enough food, assuming the fighting has ended and the 3 million to 5 million land mines dispersed around the countryside have been cleared away. The humanitarian assistance that has been provided in the refugee camps in Pakistan and Iran by the United Nations and twenty-eight international and voluntary agencies will be even more essential inside Afghanistan, as will the services of many caring volunteers, such as the French medical workers who, at great personal risk during the fighting, provided health care to both *mujahidin* and the civilian population in rural areas.

If 9,000 Soviet advisers are forced to leave because they fear for their safety, they must be replaced. They served as key officials in every ministry of the government. They commanded the Afghan army and air force. They made up two thirds of the faculty of Kabul University. They pervaded the educational system. Their departure will leave governing and political institutions barely able to function.

Some educated and experienced Afghans will return from exile, but they will not be numerous enough to fill the gap. Many of their ranks have been killed. Nor will it be easy to train Afghans to replace them. A decade of war has prevented a whole generation from getting the schooling that would prepare it to help rebuild and run the country.

Few Western development technicians and advisers are left. The United Nations Development Program still funds teacher training programs, while WHO and UNESCO continue child-care activities in Kabul but have functioned only in government-controlled zones for security reasons. Credits from the World Bank and similar institutions were suspended in 1980.

The Soviet Sphere of Influence

Expecting Afghanistan to sever its ties with the Soviet Union is probably unrealistic. The economic and military links are too strong, and Afghanistan's debt to the U.S.S.R. too large. All of the country's natural gas goes north, as does the bulk of its trade. Its military establishment is completely dependent on Soviet arms and equipment. Any attempt to do without Soviet economic support would move Afghanistan back to square one in the development game it has been playing for forty years. Moreover, world opinion generally acquiesces in considering Afghanistan within the Soviet sphere of influence.

What then would be the character of a neutral Afghanistan? So much depends on who takes charge after the Soviet troops have gone. Any future leader will find the Soviet influence deeply ingrained. An estimated 25,000 thousand Afghan young people have been educated in the U.S.S.R. in an attempt to win over a significant portion of them to communism. Within Afghanistan itself the education system has been completely transformed to the Soviet model, with the intention of creating a new progressive generation to take over the country. Communist youth organizations have been established and young people required to join teams for the preservation of public order.

Adults too have been organized into Soviet-style trade unions, designed primarily to get workers to support government policies. Women have their own Democratic Women's Organization, and farmers are supposedly represented by a Central Council of Agricultural Cooperatives. Radio and television presented a continuous barrage of communist propaganda during the war, with over half of the broadcasts on Radio Kabul actually originating from transmitters in the U.S.S.R. As the older generation died off, the Soviets expected to have enough young people indoctrinated to provide the officers and soldiers for the army, bureaucrats for the government ministries, administrators and police for the rural provinces, schoolteachers, and other key officials.

This policy required patience and persistence, but the Soviets believed that it would succeed, given sufficient time. Future Afghan governments will have to contend with the residue of this legacy and with the reality of the mighty Russian bear sitting on their northern border. Afghan leaders must understand and accept that their country can never return to the opportunistic games their predecessors played before the Saur Revolution.

Afghanistan's future holds hardship, confusion, and perhaps even chaos. Yet the Afghans will persevere, as they always have, buoyed by their belief in their ancient traditions and their inalienable rights.

One of the most encouraging developments of recent months has been a spate of *mujahid* marriages, both in the refugee camps in Pakistan and inside Afghanistan. In the earlier years of the conflict, the freedom fighters delayed permanent commitments, waiting for the end of the war. Now they are encouraging marriages and are eager to have children—their expression of their confidence in the future.

Bibliography

Ahmad, Egbal, and Richard S. Barnet. "A Reporter at Large (Afghanistan)." *The New Yorker*, Vol. LXIV, No. 8, April 11, 1988, pp. 44–86. An excellent, lively, and informed article on the invasion, power politics around the world, and prospects for the future.

Auboyer, Jeannine. *The Art of Afghanistan.* Feltham, England: Hamlyn Publishing Group, Ltd., 1968. A coffee-table book of photos of Afghan art from earliest times, with a detailed history and lengthy notes on each of the plates.

Arnold, Anthony. *Afghanistan: The Soviet Invasion in Perspective.* Stanford: Hoover Institution Press, 1981. Concise analysis of twentieth-century events in Afghanistan with a bias toward identifying Soviet economic (1960s), political (1970s), and military (1978 on) penetration of the country.

Bonner, Arthur. *Among the Afghans.* Durham, NC: Duke University Press, 1987. A penetrating analysis of the political situation during the Soviet occupation by a *New York Times* correspondent who traveled clandestinely throughout Afghanistan between 1984 and 1986.

Bradsher, Henry S. *Afghanistan and the Soviet Union.* Durham, NC: Duke University Press, 1983. Very detailed account of United States and Soviet policy relating to Afghanistan throughout the entire post–World War II period.

Chaliand, Gerard. *Report from Afghanistan* (translated from French). Harmondsworth, England: Penguin Books, 1982. Short, well-condensed account of the Soviet occupation and Afghan resistance with clear analysis of the problems and prospects.

Democratic Republic of Afghanistan. "Report on the Socio-Economic Situation; Development Strategy Assistance Needs," May 1983. Prepared for the World Bank.

Dupree, Louis. *Afghanistan.* Princeton, NJ: Princeton University Press, 1980. Ethnographic study of Afghanistan by a resident anthropologist.

———. American Universities Field Staff Reports, 1964–1979. Essays by an anthropologist working in Afghanistan on everything from saint cults to linguistics.

Fraser-Tytler, Sir William Kerr. *Afghanistan.* London: Oxford University Press, 1967. Classic British study of history and political developments in Afghanistan by an English colonial official.

Girardet, Edward R. *Afghanistan: The Soviet War.* New York: St. Martin's Press, 1985. Description and analysis by a journalist who has made several clandestine trips into Afghanistan, concentrating on the impact of the Soviet invasion on the country.

Griffiths, John C. *Afghanistan: Key to a Continent.* Boulder, CO: Westview Press, 1981. Somewhat dated political and economic analysis of Afghanistan in the 1960s and 1970s.

Hammond, Thomas T. *Red Flag over Afghanistan.* Boulder, CO: Westview Press, 1984. Excellent analysis of the Communist coup in Afghanistan and Soviet foreign policy, by an academic.

Hyman, Anthony. *Afghanistan under Soviet Domination, 1964–83.* London: The Macmillan Press Ltd., 1984. Detailed and thoughtful analysis of the events that fostered the growth of the Afghan opposition to the communist takeover and Soviet occupation.

International Institute for Strategic Studies. *Strategic Survey, 1986–1987.* London: International Institute for Strategic Studies, 1987. Annual review of the military situation in the Soviet Union and Afghanistan.

International Monetary Fund. *Direction of Trade Statistics Yearbook 1986.* Washington: International Monetary Fund, 1987.

Michaud, Roland and Sabrina. *Afghanistan: Paradise Lost.* New York: Vendome Press, 1985. Excellent color photos of Afghanistan.

Middle East Journal. Chronology: Afghanistan, 1972–1987.

Spain, James W. *The Way of the Pathans.* London: Robert Hale Ltd., 1962. Detailed description of Pushtun culture and customs.

United Nations General Assembly. "Situation of human rights in Afghanistan," November 1985.

United States Department of State. Bureau of Public Affairs. *Background Notes: Afghanistan, July 1986* (published periodically). Excellent short review.

————. "Afghanistan: Eight Years of Soviet Occupation," December 1987. Published annually. Excellent short summary of the current situation in Afghanistan.

————. "Soviet Influence on Afghan Youth," February 1986. A review of Soviet domination of the Afghan education system and youth activities.

Additional Resources

Biography

Lamb, Harold. *Tamerlane, the Earth Shaker.* Garden City, NY: Garden City Publishing Company, Inc., 1928. Nonfiction account of the Central Asian warrior by a well-known British biographer.

———. *Alexander the Great.* New York: Doubleday & Company, Inc., 1946. Nonfiction account of the young Macedonian general who conquered most of the known world.

Biography (Juvenile)

Demi. *The Adventures of Marco Polo.* New York: Holt, Rinehart and Winston, Inc., 1982.

Greene, Carol. *Marco Polo: Voyager to the Orient.* Chicago: Children's Press, 1987.

Preston, Edna Mitchell. *Marco Polo: a Story of the Middle Ages.* New York: Crowell-Collier Press, 1968.

Description (Current)

Stegmuller, Camille. *Afghanistan in Pictures.* New York: Sterling Publishing Co., 1971. Description for juveniles of land, history, government, people, economy; with photos.

Spiegleman, Judith M. *Shaer of Afghanistan.* New York: Julian Messner, 1969. Nonfiction account for juveniles of a day in the life of an Afghan boy; with photos.

Fiction

Caldwell, Taylor. *The Earth Is the Lord's: A Tale of the Rise of Genghis Khan.* New York: The Literary Guild of America, 1940. Novel about the Mongol warlord's building of an empire.

Druon, Maurice. *Alexander, the God.* New York: Charles Scribner's Sons, 1960. Fictionalized account of Alexander's exploits, as told by his scribe.

Follett, Ken. *Lie Down with Lions.* New York: William Morrow and Company, Inc., 1986. Racy mystery involving an American woman married to a French doctor working behind the resistance lines in Afghanistan. The doctor turns out to be a Russian agent, and a CIA man rescues the girl.

Hoover, Thomas. *The Moghul.* Garden City, NY: Doubleday & Company, Inc., 1983. Novel involving the East India Company in the time of the Moghul emperors.

Kaye, M. M. *The Far Pavilions.* New York: St. Martin's Press, 1978. An Englishman brought up as an Indian becomes a secret agent for the British colonial government, ending up in Afghanistan during the Second Afghan War. The Afghans are, unfortunately, the bad guys.

Kessel, Joseph. *The Horsemen.* New York: Farrar, Straus & Giroux, 1968. Dramatic story about the men of Afghan Turkistan who raise horses and play the national game of buzkashi.

Lloyd-Jones, Robin. *Lord of the Dance.* Boston: Little, Brown and Company, 1983. Two Englishmen have adventures in sixteenth-century India while the Moghuls are ruling.

Marshall, Edison. *Caravan to Xanadu: A Novel of Marco Polo.* New York: Farrar, Straus & Young, Inc., 1953. Marco Polo's adventures, by a well-known novelist.

Michener, James. *Caravans.* New York: Random House, Inc., 1963. A twentieth-century novel in the usual Michener grand style, set in Afghanistan. Afghans will tell you that the American woman could not have traveled with the tribes as she did in the book.

Renault, Mary. *Fire from Heaven.* New York: Pantheon Books, Inc., 1969. *The Persian Boy.* New York: Pantheon Books, Inc., 1972. *Funeral Games.* New York: Pantheon Books, Inc., 1981. Trilogy covering the life of Alexander the Great in great detail.

Wright, Daphne. *The Distant Kingdom.* New York: Delacorte Press, 1987. English colonial and military life in India, ending up in Kabul during the First Afghan War. Here again the Afghans are, unfortunately, the bad guys.

For Younger Readers

Jennings, Gary. *The Journeyer.* New York: Atheneum Publishers, 1984. Novel about Marco Polo's travels.

History

Carroll, David. *The Taj Mahal.* New York: Newsweek, 1973. Profusely illustrated presentation of the Moghul Empire, including the Taj Mahal.

Dunn, Ross E. *The Adventures of Ibn Battuta: A Moslem Traveler of the 14th Century.* Berkeley: University of California Press, 1986. Account of twenty-nine years of a pilgrim/scholar's journeying, from his home in Morocco to Central Asia and China.

Latham, Ronald. *The Travels of Marco Polo.* New York: Abaris Books, 1958. Condensed and attractively presented version of Marco Polo's very long personal account of his travels.

History (Juvenile)

Ceserani, Gian Paolo. *Marco Polo.* New York: G. P. Putnam's Sons, 1982. Delightfully illustrated short account of Marco Polo's adventures.

Rawding, F. W. *The Buddha.* Minneapolis: Lerner Publications Co., 1979. Presentation of Buddhism, with a short section on Asoka.

Rugoff, Milton Allen. *Marco Polo's Adventures in China.* New York: American Heritage Publishing Company, Inc., 1964. Detailed history with profuse illustrations.

Winsing, Robert and Nancy. *Ancient India and its Influence in Modern Times.* New York: Franklin Watts, 1973. History of India, with good section on Buddhism and the Mauryan Empire.

Travel

Newby, Eric. *A Short Walk through the Hindu Kush.* Harmondsworth, England: Penguin Books, 1968. Two Englishmen use mountain climbing as an excuse to penetrate the remote Afghan province of Nuristan; a witty travel account.

Severin, Tim. *Tracking Marco Polo.* New York: Peter Bedrick Books, 1964. Three young Englishmen on two motorcycles travel from Oxford to Venice, then follow Marco Polo's route across the Middle East and Afghanistan.

Index

References to illustrations are in *italics*.